∽ INTRODUCTION ∽

For those who know me well, it's no surprise that I get a serious amount of joy from planning parties. Growing up in a close knit family, birthdays and holiday celebrations were some of the most anticipated events of the year—a time to gather friends and family together, to "ooh" and "ahh" over themed decorations, savor a delicious meal and spend time together. The women in my life are all great hostesses, so I would like to think entertaining is in my blood. When most young 20-somethings were planning their nightlife for the weekend, I was planning dinner parties to host in my tiny one-bedroom apartment. And once my friends began getting married and starting their own families, my focus quickly shifted to planning festive birthday parties. I became "Auntie Kelly" to almost twenty children over the last ten years. It's a title that I hold with honor and has been one of the greatest joys of my life thus far. These little people have given me so much happiness over the years, including countless reasons to celebrate!

After a wonderful stint in the fashion industry, my focus suddenly shifted to the entertaining world. In 2009, I launched the popular lifestyle and entertaining blog, *The Party Dress*, and quickly grew a following of like-minded hostesses. People come to my blog for ideas they can recreate for their events—from DIY party decorations to that perfect cocktail recipe. I'm fortunate to work with an amazing group of clients to help them plan unique events, from kids' parties to baby showers, bridal showers and even holiday events.

My social stationery company, WH Hostess, designs modern party invitations and paper goods that you will see used throughout this book. For me, a party's design starts with the invitation, and I strive to create invitations that can inspire an entire theme.

It's likely that I have one of the happiest jobs in the world—designing, crafting and styling special celebrations for my friends, family and amazing clients. I was thrilled with the opportunity to share my love for parties with you by creating this book. I have a passion for creating extraordinary events for children.

Creating a stylish, modern interpretation of a classic party theme, or a fresh take on the latest trend, is what really gets my creative juices flowing. I like to create an experience for the child and their guests by designing an event that the kids will love, but that also appeals to the parents' design aesthetic.

My goal in writing this resource for stylish kids' parties was to fill it to the brim with eye-candy, but also to include practical information and tips that will help make these ideas attainable for your parties.

This book contains twelve chapters, each full of ideas for a different theme party—baby showers, first birthdays, kids' parties and even a couple of holiday celebrations. The theme possibilities for kids' parties are just about endless. I wanted to make sure that the ideas I shared in this book today would be just as valid twenty years from now. You will find current interpretations of classic party themes, with instructions on how to execute special décor projects, ideas for serving food and desserts, styling an on-trend dessert table, and tips for carrying out a theme from start to finish. It's all about the details—all of the little projects add up to create one gorgeous, big-picture idea.

I hope you enjoy the book and find it a useful resource in planning your children's events for years to come!

HERE
comes
TROUBLE
· baby ware arrives ·
MARCH 2013

SWEET
BABY
WARE

Renewals

KELLY ROHLFS LYDEN

CONTENTS

For my mother, who has been present at every important occasion in my life. She taught me that above all, a good hostess always holds herself to a standard of grace, not perfection.

Look for this symbol throughout the book to find projects and party elements that feature a template found in the Templates section.

1

BABY CHIC

baby shower

THE ANTICIPATION OF A NEW BABY is one of life's greatest joys and deserves to be celebrated in style. Although there are many popular themes for modern baby showers, I believe you can throw a chic party that reflects the mama-to-be's design aesthetic, while incorporating classic baby icons.

When it came time to throw my sister's baby shower, I decided to do just that. I used a fresh color palette of aqua and coral, mixed with a touch of shimmer and classic baby items: rattles, baby blocks and storks. With a few simple do-it-yourself craft projects, a spectacular dessert table and the perfect balance of modern and classic ideas, I hope this party gives you ideas to incorporate into any baby shower.

SETTING *the* THEME

When getting started, I like to direct my attention to one main focal point in each room of the party. For this shower, I chose to include the fireplace décor, the dessert table and the table settings. The fireplace served as a backdrop for gift opening, so guests would be looking at it for quite some time. I created custom art prints to place on the mantel, surrounded by bouquets of tulips and roses in monochromatic arrangements. A double-strung garland of braided satin ribbon soared across the top of the fireplace, and mini clothespins held a variety of patterned onesies.

Invitation

The invitation to any event is the first impression—so make it a fabulous one! I think it is important that it reflect the color palette, the level of formality and the theme for the event. For this baby shower, the classic stork was updated with a crisp, striped shirt and polka dot scarf, and looked fresh against a tonal aqua blue chevron background.

Rattle Floral Decor

Welcome guests into the baby shower with a statement piece. To create the look of a whimsical, oversized rattle, I used two different sizes of floral foam balls, an empty paper towel roll, ribbon and daisies. This project was very simple to put together, and if using fresh flowers, should be done just before the start of the party. It could also be constructed using silk flowers and repurposed as nursery décor after the event.

Braided Garland

One of my favorite go-to party décor ideas is the ribbon garland. You can select ribbons that are color-coordinated to your event to create the custom braided garland. For major impact, I like hanging them double-strung. And since ribbon is extremely lightweight, the garland can be secured on just about anything.

Chair Sign

My sister's chair held a special "Mama-to-be" sign, identifying her seat at the head table. It also added a touch of pattern and décor to the space.

Centerpieces with Shimmer

Glitter-embellished vases held large bouquets of coral roses, tulips and white hydrangeas. To incorporate a touch of shimmer, I dressed up basic glass rose bowls with glittered polka dots. Simple to create, this is an idea you could use for any party! Just dip a removable glue dot into any shade of glitter and then apply to the vase.

◢ Placecards and Game

Instead of using a traditional tent card to identify guests' seats, I created a classic baby rattle placecard (found in the Templates section) that can be personalized and cut out. Weave it between the prongs of a fork to make it stand at each place setting.

A Celebrity Baby Name Game icebreaker card (found in the Templates section) was color-coordinated and included a white, personalized pencil. The game was a great way to encourage guests to interact.

A Gorgeous Tablesetting

For this baby shower, I set up a series of round tables with white rental chairs. Crisp, white tablecloths were the perfect backdrop to my gorgeous centerpieces and colorful place settings. Basic white china, silverware and footed water glasses gave the table a more elegant feel. A coral napkin was placed under the plate for a pop of color against the white tablecloth.

DESSERTS *and* DETAILS

To give the dessert table a pop of modern glam, I used a chevron sequin tablecloth as the base. It played off the shimmer from the polka-dot centerpieces and made for a gorgeous backdrop for all of the desserts. I used mainly white plates and cake stands for a uniform look, embellishing them all with coordinating patterned Cake Plate Clings. Aqua tent cards resembling ribbon identified the treats, and two 36" (91cm) balloons helped to define the vertical space above the table.

Fete-Worthy Food

Playing host to a room full of women can be a daunting task, especially if you are cooking and serving food, refilling drinks and trying to be a social butterfly! Ladies tend to prefer lighter meal options, especially at lunchtime. For this event, I served a few salads, my homemade popovers with strawberry butter, and set up a quiche bar featuring four different flavors. It was the perfect amount of food, and everything could be made prior to the event, so I was able to quickly set up the buffet without being away from my guests for too long. I suggest labeling your food with tent cards (found in the Templates section) to identify the food. Not only will it add a touch of décor to your table, but it's also very helpful to guests with food allergies.

Embellish Your Drinks

No matter what your drink of choice is, it's always better with a festive straw. Stripes, polka dots and more are available in paper straw form now from our favorite party resource. Dress them up with our straw flags template (found in the Templates section), so they exclaim "Cheers to the Mama!" and "Oh Baby".

Creative Cocktails

Baby showers are a fabulous opportunity to get creative with your cocktails (or mocktails for the mama-to-be). Citrus water is one of my go-to entertaining secrets. A beautiful drink dispenser of water can be flavored with sliced lemons, strawberries and mint for a refreshing nonalcoholic option, while a mimosa bar featuring champagne and different fruit nectar mixers is the perfect luncheon treat.

Bite-Size Desserts

A dessert table not only serves as a beautiful focal point for your event, but can also offer guests sweet treats to enjoy at the party or to bring home with them. During a baby shower, guests often sit for a while watching the mama-to-be open her gifts, and a dessert table is a great way to encourage them to get up and help themselves. I find that bite-size desserts are best, so guests can try more than one. Mini lemon, key lime or chocolate tarts, cake pops and brownie bites are among my go-to dessert options.

Embellish Your Cupcakes

Cupcakes are a go-to party food, whether you are serving two-year-olds or sixty-year-olds. I'm all for baking, but often I find that I have to pick and choose what I am going to make myself and what I am going to outsource. Store-bought cupcakes can easily be dressed up to look couture! A patterned cupcake wrapper can tie the treat into your theme, and fondant toppers are a great way to customize them. These darling toppers feature baby shoes and a tonal chevron pattern.

Personalize Your Sweets

Add a touch of personalization to your dessert offerings by incorporating the baby's initials. I asked one of my favorite cookie designers, Allyson Jane, to create these precious onesie cookies featuring a *W* for the baby's last name initial. I also incorporated the phrase "Oh, baby" into the fondant banner across the cake and on the cake pop rattles.

Baby Blocks

Baby blocks are a classic staple when it comes to nursery décor or baby shower decorations. I wanted to incorporate them into my dessert table, but had a difficult time sourcing blocks that would coordinate with my unusual color palette. I decided to make them myself using custom paper, wood blocks and découpage glue. Although they look darling stacked up, you can also repurpose the boxes on your buffet table. I stacked a basic white plate on the largest block to create a custom cake stand.

TASSEL GARLAND

Jump on board with one of today's hottest trends with this simple DIY project: the tissue paper tassel garland. You can color-coordinate this project for any event, and the garland can be used in a variety of ways: decorating a fireplace mantel, strung on a dessert table, or hanging from jumbo balloons as festive décor.

SUPPLIES:

tissue paper · scissors · ribbon · double-stick tape or glue

1 With one piece of tissue paper laid flat, fold in half along the longest side.

2 Fold the strip in half, and then in half again.

3 Starting at the bottom (unfolded side), cut strips about $1/2$" (13mm) in width. Do not cut all the way through to the top—be sure to leave at least 1"–2" (3cm–5cm) at the top.

4 Open up the piece of tissue paper so it is laying flat again. Starting at one side, roll the piece horizontally, as tight as you can (the cut sides should be facing out to either side).

5 Once your piece of tissue paper is completely rolled up, twist the very center of the roll. As you continue to twist, the center will start to bend into a loop. Use a piece of double-stick tape or a drop of glue to hold the loop together.

6 Once you have created all of your tassels, string them onto ribbon to hang.

CAKE POP RATTLES

Cake Recipe

INGREDIENTS

1 cup (225g) white granulated sugar

$^1/_2$ cup (110g) butter, softened

2 eggs

2 tsps. vanilla extract

1$^1/_2$ cups (165g) all-purpose flour

1$^3/_4$ tsps. baking powder

$^1/_2$ cup (120mL) milk

DIRECTIONS

Preheat oven to 350°F. (180°C or gas mark 4). Grease and flour a 9"×9" (23cm × 23cm) or 9"×13" (23cm × 33cm) pan.

In a medium bowl, whisk together the sugar and butter. Beat in the eggs, one at a time, and then stir in the vanilla extract. In a separate bowl, combine flour and baking powder. Add this mixture to the sugar and butter and mix well. Finally, slowly stir in the milk until the batter is smooth. Pour batter into the prepared pan.

Bake for 30–40 minutes in a preheated oven. The cake is done when it springs back to the touch. Allow the cake to cool completely before starting the cake pop steps.

Sweet Baby Ware was born April 1, 2013. Welcome to the family, Benjamin Amos!

Cake Pops

SUPPLIES

crumbled cake • buttercream frosting • chocolate melts • candy coloring set (optional) • 4"–6" (10cm–15cm) lollipop sticks • Styrofoam form

DIRECTIONS

1 Crumble your prebaked cake into a large bowl.

2 Mix in ¾ of a container of store-bought buttercream frosting into the bowl. Combine thoroughly.

3 Using a small ice cream scoop, scoop the mixture into your hands and roll into a ball. Place the finished balls on a pan, spaced about an inch (3cm) apart. Once all of the balls are rolled, place the pan in the freezer for about 10–15 minutes to chill.

4 Warm your chocolate melts according to the manufacturer's instructions. You can buy pre-made colors, or use candy dye kits to create your own custom color. Once the chocolate is melted, pull your pan of cake balls out of the freezer.

5 Dip one end of a lollipop stick into the melted chocolate and insert it into a cake ball. Repeat with all of the cake balls, and place the pan back in the freezer for another 10–15 minutes.

6 Dip a chilled cake pop into the melted chocolate in one quick swoop. After the entire ball is covered with chocolate, gently shake the stick to allow any excess chocolate to fall off back into the bowl.

7 Stand the cake pop up using a Styrofoam form to allow drying evenly. Once dry, follow the instructions for assembling your rattles.

Cake Pop Rattles

SUPPLIES

cake pops • chocolate melts • premade white fondant • candy coloring set (optional) • paper straws • ribbon • piping bag and tip

DIRECTIONS

Use these steps to turn your basic cake pops into baby rattles—the perfect addition to any baby shower dessert table.

Place a paper straw over the lollipop stick of a completed cake pop, and cut the length so it is slightly shorter than the stick. Attach a small ball of fondant at the bottom to hold the straw in place. Dip the fondant ball end into the melted chocolate and tap off any excess just like you did with the cake pop end. Allow the fondant end to dry completely. Using a piping bag and tip, pipe a seal of chocolate around each end of the straw and add chocolate decoration to the ball of the rattle. I suggest polka dots, chevrons, stripes, the baby's initial or a cute phrase like "Oh, baby!" After the chocolate piping dries, tie a ribbon on the stick for additional decoration.

resources

Paper goods, art prints, Celebrity Baby Name Game, Cake Plate Clings (whhostess.com); ribbon, glue dots, chocolate melts, candy dye kit (michaels.com, hobbylobby.com or joanns.com); personalized white pencils (orientaltrading.com); tissue paper (containerstore.com); sequin chevron tablecloth (latavolalinens.com); découpage glue and square forms (paper-source.com); fondant cake banner, cupcake toppers (lynleespetitecakes.com); sugar cookies (allysonjane.com); 36" (91cm) balloons, paper straws (shopsweetlulu.com).

2

WHAT WILL IT BEE?

baby shower

WHEN THROWING A BABY SHOWER for a couple who wants to remain in the dark about the gender of their baby, it's important to choose a gender-neutral color palette and a theme that appeals to the parents' design aesthetic.

A bumble bee theme is a classic choice for a baby shower or a child's birthday party, and is typically executed in a crisp yellow, black and white color story. To bring a fresh approach to this classic theme, swap out the black for a French blue and add in some preppy provincial touches, such as textile mixing with a clover pattern and a tight stripe.

This party was inspired by the Bumble Bee Topiary collection from WH Hostess, which combines these playful patterns, along with a lemon topiary tree and a classic bumble bee icon. These charming elements can be repeated throughout the party décor to create a cohesive look for your mama-to-bee. Follow along for creative ideas and do-it-yourself projects designed to help you re-create this theme.

SETTING *the* THEME

When creating an inviting table setting for adult guests, I often rely on layering textures and components to style a look that is sure to delight. The crisp, white location for our "What will it bee?" baby shower really made our French blue and yellow color palette pop. White Chivari chairs sidled up next to tables dressed in tablecloths made from a textured white fabric. The modern chain link pattern is one that I use frequently to infuse texture into tables or backdrops. I layered navy blue charger plates, white china and basic silverware onto the table, and accessorized it with blue goblets.

Napkins were dressed up with personalized honeycomb placecards and a yellow grosgrain ribbon. You can re-create this look by using the templates (found in the Templates section) and simple DIY project instructions in the following pages.

To balance out our pop colors on the table, I created a simple centerpiece by using grocery-store items. Produce is an affordable option, and looks chic and modern when styled en masse. I placed a bowl full of lemons, with a few boxwood leaf sprigs stuck in for a pop of green, in the center of the table, along with white ginger jars for added texture.

Invite Your Guests in Style

The invitations should express your theme, color palette and give an indication of formality. Make sure they are printed in full color on a luxe cardstock. If you are hand-delivering your invitations, you can also get creative in the accompaniments. For this theme, I would suggest pairing the invitation with a tin of French lemon candies, or perhaps tying the invitation to the stem of a boxwood topiary tree.

Baby Bingo Game

Guests often remain seated at their tables while the guest of honor opens her gifts. It can be fun to engage the guests in a simple game during this time, such as baby bingo (found in the Templates section). You can find options online that you can print off, or custom stationers can create a color-coordinated version for you.

Menu Card

A hanging menu card (found in the Templates section) is a colorful way to dress up the white Chivari chairs and also inform guests of the details of the meal they are about to enjoy.

Sip in Style
Whether it's a cocktail, a mocktail (nonalcoholic for the mama-to-bee) or just a party staple like lemonade or iced tea, you can continue your party theme into a signature drink, complete with coordinating accessories. For this party, lemonade was served up with a dash of honey, a sprig of mint leaves and a wooden honey stick—delicious and stylish!

It's All in the Details
Carrying the details throughout your party décor will help you create a cohesive party. For this theme, we used lemons as a detail to reference the lemon topiary tree on the invitation, and also to infuse the bright yellow color throughout the entire party. Produce can be a great, affordable centerpiece for any party. Take a peek around your grocery store for inspiration that can work with just about any color palette.

Party Favors
A little pot of honey is the perfect take-home treat for guests to remember this special event. Dress up your jar with a fabric or paper embellishment on the lid and a customized label.

HONEYCOMB PLACECARDS

SUPPLIES

 honeycomb placecard template (found in the Templates section) • scissors or craft knife • straightedge • ribbon • cutting mat

1 Photocopy the honeycomb template (found in the Templates section) as many times as needed. Cut out the honeycomb place-cards and write your guests' names on them. Using a straightedge and a craft knife, cut a small $1/2$" (13mm) slit at each side of the placecard.

2 Cut a 6" (15cm) piece of ribbon and weave it through the slits. Repeat with the remaining placecards.

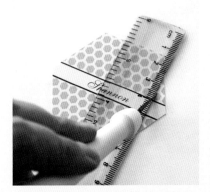

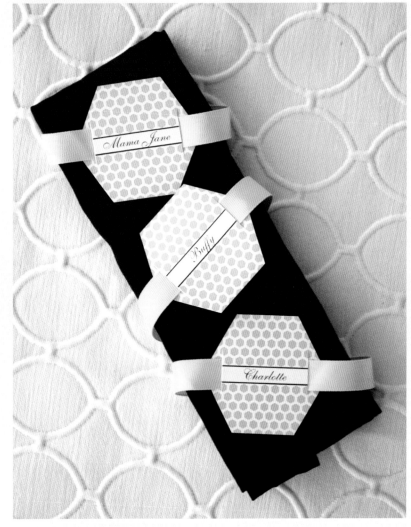

DESSERTS *and* DETAILS

Desserts are not only delicious, but a well-styled table can serve as a main decoration for your party space. It's a great way to pull together all of the elements of your party in one gorgeous surprise.

For this party, a simple white tablecloth was enhanced with a clover-patterned square topper in the French blue and yellow color palette. I covered a large board with the white textured fabric that was used for tablecloths on our lunch tables to serve as the table's backdrop. This allowed the yellow candy and desserts to really stand out, and created a sense of continuity with the other tables in the room.

All white and glass serving pieces were used to highlight the array of yellow candy. I dressed up the cake stands with Cake Plate Clings in coordinating patterns to add a pop of pattern. The monochromatic candy was displayed in either glass apothecary jars or stacked on cake stands. To tie in with the lemon element of the party, all of the candies were lemon-flavored.

Some of the dessert highlights included a lemon mousse cake, mini cupcakes with flags that asked "What will it bee?," honeycomb-shaped cookies with tiny sugar bee decorations, and darling bumble bee cake pops. I baked a beehive-shaped Bundt cake that was then drizzled with white royal icing and embellished with some sugar bee decorations. My favorite dessert of the afternoon was my honeycomb-shaped lemon tarts. One of my go-to recipes for parties, I revamped the tart crust to be a hexagon shape. When laid out together on a serving tray, they look just like a honeycomb!

Cake Pops

Cake pops are one of my favorite dessert table trends. Easy to eat, cake pops are little pieces of art, and are a great way to carry a pattern or theme throughout your desserts. These delightful bee pops were made using chocolate melts as the wings. Looking for a way to display cake pops? Fill a vase with candy and stand them up…it will show them off perfectly!

Beehive Bundt Cake

A Bundt cake is one of the easiest cakes to make and decorate! Gourmet specialty stores carry a variety of shaped pans, so you can really coordinate your cake to your party. This beehive-shaped cake was embellished with a thick royal icing dribble and some sweet bee sugar decorations.

Yellow Candy

Tiered serving pieces can make for an interesting candy display! I stacked up varieties of yellow candy for this display, making a footed bowl full of rock candy sticks the centerpiece.

HONEYCOMB MINI LEMON TARTS

Honeycomb Tart Shell

INGREDIENTS

1¼ sticks (150g) unsalted butter, at room temperature

½ cup (110g) sugar

½ tsp. pure vanilla extract

1½ cups (165g) all-purpose flour

pinch salt

DIRECTIONS

In the bowl of an electric mixer, mix together butter and sugar with a paddle attachment. Once combined, add the vanilla. In a medium bowl, sift together the flour and salt, then slowly add them to the butter and sugar mixture. Mix on low speed until the dough starts to combine. Wrap the dough in plastic wrap and place in the refrigerator to chill for 30 minutes, or until firm.

Once the dough is chilled, remove from the refrigerator and unwrap the plastic wrap. Lightly dust your countertop or cutting board with flour, and then roll out the dough using a rolling pin until it is approximately ¼" (6mm) thick. Use a hexagon-shaped cookie cutter to cut out the dough. Once cut, gently fold over each side of the hexagon to create the tart shell walls. Place the tart shells onto a baking sheet and brush with an egg wash. Bake at 350°F (180°C or gas mark 4) for 15–20 minutes, or until lightly browned. Remove from the oven and let cool.

Lemon Curd

INGREDIENTS

2 lemons, at room temperature

1 cup (225g) sugar

$^1/_2$ stick (110g) unsalted butter, at room temperature

2 extra-large eggs, at room temperature

pinch of salt

DIRECTIONS

Remove the zest from one lemon using a zester, and squeeze both lemons to make $^1/_4$ cup (60mL) of juice; set the juice aside.

In a food processor fitted with a steel blade, combine the lemon zest and the sugar, and whisk until the zest is very fine. In the bowl of an electric mixer fitted with a paddle attachment, cream the butter with the zest and sugar mixture. Add the eggs, lemon juice and salt, and mix until combined.

Cook the mixture over low heat in a saucepan, stirring constantly, until thickened (about 10 minutes). Remove from the heat once the lemon curd reaches 175°F (79°C).

Fill the tart shell with warm lemon curd and allow to set at room temperature. Top off tarts with a single blueberry just before serving.

3

PINWHEELS & POLKA DOTS

first birthday party

A FIRST BIRTHDAY IS A HUGE MILESTONE in a family, and definitely deserves a party! Since the guest of honor is just a mere twelve months old, the party is generally geared towards the adults and older children in the baby's life. It's a wonderful opportunity to gather friends and family to celebrate both the magic of that first year, and also congratulate the parents for making it through in one piece!

When selecting a theme for a first birthday, I like to work off a baby's favorite toy, a classic book or a child's nickname and then add modern design elements to create a sophisticated design. Pinwheels are a fabulous option, as their movement captures a little one's attention. They are also very simple to construct, making them the perfect party décor!

SETTING THEME

With a nod to the pinwheel's classic heritage, plan your décor around playful polka dots and simple stripes to create a festive party space. I wanted this party to be perfectly preppy, just like the birthday girl, Sara Jane. A color palette of pinks and blues was born; however, all of these ideas could be replicated with a variety of color palettes—aqua and orange, lime green and pink, or navy blue and green.

When starting the planning process for any party, I select three to four main ideas or areas on which to focus my attention. For this event, those areas included the party entrance, a creative photo booth backdrop, simple décor to dress up my party space, and a festive dessert table featuring a fabulous cake. Planning ahead helps me streamline my focus to the areas that will make the biggest impact.

Entrance

Welcome your guests to your party with a colorful doorway by dressing it with tissue decorations. I layered multiple sizes of tissue fans in pink and blue with some of my handcrafted pinwheels to create an entrance that screams "The party is HERE!" Attach the decorations with adhesive putty or removable plastic hooks, both found at your local craft or hardware store.

Simple Décor

Carry out the pinwheels and polka dots theme by infusing polka dots throughout your party décor. Pinwheels crafted with scrapbook paper, polka dot ribbon and extra-fancy balloons make this party extra special. Pinwheels are a great DIY project because you can scale them to any size. One of my favorite details from this party is a mini 3-D pinwheel on the invitation. The instructions are found on the next page.

Confetti Balloons

Nothing says "party" quite like balloons. With patterned options, jumbo-sized, and (my current obsession) clear, there are so many creative ways to have fun with balloons that you rarely see a cluster of plain old balloons anymore. I love the endless opportunities that clear balloons give a hostess. My favorite option is to fill them with colorful confetti prior to adding the helium. It's a great way to bring a few more polka dots to this theme.

PINWHEEL AND INVITATION

◀ The steps used to create the mini pinwheels for the invitation can be scaled to create larger pinwheels for overall décor or the photo booth backdrop.

SUPPLIES

squares of double-sided scrapbook paper • scissors • brackets • lollipop sticks • single hole punch • jewels • hot glue gun • invitations (found in the Templates section) • pinwheel template (found in the Templates section) • ribbon

1 Using the pinwheel template (found in the Templates section), cut a square from double-sided scrapbook paper. Cut a slit from each corner of your square, being sure not to cut all the way to the center.

2 Fold a corner in toward the center. Repeat with the remaining three corners.

3 Press a bracket through the center of the pinwheel, securing all four corners. Once pulled through to the back of the pinwheel, open the bracket's ends and wrap them around a lollipop stick. You can insert a dab of hot glue to hold the stick in place. Embellish the center of your pinwheel with an oversized, craft-store jewel. Attach it with a small dab of hot glue.

4 Punch two holes in the invitation (found in the Templates section) and weave a 6" (15cm) piece of ribbon through them. Tie the pinwheel to the card with the ribbon.

PARTY FAVOR BAGS

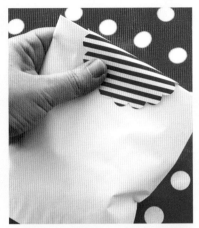

Deliver your party favors in style by placing them on a Lucite tray embellished with ribbon and a pinwheel. Simple white bags can be dressed up with ribbon, and can hold anything from small trinkets to candy or baked goods.

SUPPLIES

3" (8cm) scallop craft punch · scrapbook paper · hole punch · ¼" (6mm) ribbon · paper bags

1 Using a 3" (8cm) scallop craft punch, punch out one scrapbook paper circle for each bag.

2 Fold the circle in half. Fill your paper bags with party favors, and fold the top over (toward the back).

3 Place the folded circle over the top fold of the bag. Punch two holes about ½" (13mm) apart. Weave the ribbon through the holes and tie in a bow.

DESSERTS *and* DETAILS

Preppy stripes, polka dots and a classic color palette are a killer combination for any birthday party. Throw in a key textile (I used ribbon) to repeat throughout the space to create a cohesive look, and the end result will be absolutely perfect. The dessert table is the perfect place to pull together all of your design elements to show off your theme in style. A hot pink tonal polka dot fabric backdrop was used to make the desserts stand out, and a tablecloth brought stripes into the mix. White cake stands and platters were used to hold color-coordinated desserts and candy, with the pinwheel cake holding center stage.

Chair Décor

Rental chairs are typically a necessity when entertaining a crowd, and I find that adding a touch of personality to simple white folding or Chivari chairs can make a big impact on the look of a party. For this event, I tied scraps of ribbons in coordinating colors of pink and blue around the top bar of the chair and let them hang down. I gathered them in the middle and attached a pinwheel as an accent, which was a nod to our theme, plus it's very simple and inexpensive to do. You could also re-create this look with strips of scrap fabric.

Napkins

If you are serving a buffet-style meal, make life simple for your guests by wrapping up the silverware in napkins, making it easy for them to grab on their way to their table. You don't need to invest in fifty napkin rings! Use ribbon in coordinating colors and patterns to tie around the napkin/silverware bundles for a festive look.

Spectacular Cake

A birthday cake is one of the many important "firsts" in your child's life, and I think that not only should the cake be fabulous, but it should also serve as the centerpiece for an eye-catching dessert table. On the next page, I'll show you ways to dress up a simple store-bought cake with fondant pinwheels.

FONDANT PINWHEEL CAKE DECORATION

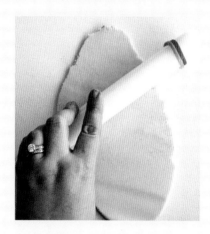
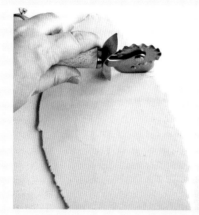

SUPPLIES

precolored fondant · party picks
or toothpicks · straightedge ·
pastry cutter · fondant rolling pin
· water · pastry brush

1 Roll out your fondant until it is
about ¹⁄₈" (3mm) thick.

2 Using a straightedge and
pastry cutter, cut out a square
(size can vary depending on your
desired look).

3 Cut in from each corner, being
sure not to cut all the way to
the center.

4 Fold in one corner and attach
it to the center with a touch of
water (apply gently with the pastry
brush). Repeat with each of the
four corners.

5 Once all four corners are folded
in, stick a party pick or embellished
toothpick in the center. Place the
pinwheel on a raised cooling rack
to dry overnight. Attach to the
cake just before the party.

Meringues

Meringues are a sugary treat that both easy to make and extremely versatile—you can adjust the color to suit your specific needs. Patterned candy cups serve as a fabulous, easy-to-grab container for meringues, candy or fruit.

Cake Pops

Cake pops are one of the best party trends to have emerged in the last few years. They're cute, they are simple to make, and you can customize them to coordinate with any theme. They are also simple two-bite desserts, making them ideal for kids and a great addition to a dessert table.

Pink Candy

There is something perfectly magical about a table full of pretty, pink candy—especially for little girls! Whether you stack it on cake stands, use it to fill up glass jars, or hand out goodie bags full of it, you can't go wrong with pink candy!

Cupcake Pompoms

Dress up store-bought cupcakes with a simple pompom food pick. Available in tons of colors at your local party goods store, you can perfectly coordinate your toppers to your specific color palette.

Photo Booth Backdrop

Birthday parties naturally create an opportunity for fun family pictures. Encourage guests to snap away by creating a colorful backdrop to pose in front of with the birthday child. For best results, select a space with natural light, and decorate the wall from top to bottom to accommodate your tallest and smallest guests. For this theme, we created dozens of pinwheels out of coordinating scrapbook paper and glued jewels in the centers for a little touch of bling.

Lollipops for the Littles
Need a way to get your little ones to pose in front of the pinwheel photo booth wall? Lollipops work every time! Petite pops make a great prize for a game or (dare I say) bribe for taking those cute family photos!

resources

Paper tissue fans (shopsweetlulu. com); patterned scrapbook paper, brackets, lollipop sticks for invitation, assortment of ribbons (michaels. com, hobbylobby.com, joanns.com, papersource.com); navy blue and pink cloth napkins (homegoods. com); clear balloons, confetti, metallic party picks, striped popcorn boxes (partycity.com); paper goods, Cake Plate Clings (whhostess.com); precolored fondant, fondant rolling pin, fondant tools (michaels.com, hobbylobby.com, joanns.com); pink candy and lollipops (candyware-house.com); navy polka dot paper cups (shopsweetlulu.com); cake pops (sweetlaurencakes.com).

4

LITTLE MAN

first birthday party

EVERY LITTLE BOY has affectionately been referred to as a cute "little man" at least once in his first year. So why not plan a first birthday celebration around that theme? Mix together design elements like mustaches and bow ties with classic haberdashery patterns, such as gingham check and stripes for a classic, handsome party.

First birthday celebrations come in many different forms. You can throw a large party on the weekend with friends and family members—a full-blown event with all the trimmings. Or you can plan an intimate gathering for just your closest family on a weeknight—a sweet celebration with just a few special touches. This chapter will share ideas for crafting a unique celebration, whether big or small.

SETTING *the* THEME

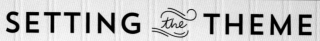

This Little Man party celebrates the first birthday of my smiley friend, John Andrew. With his charming good looks, he is downright dapper in a bow tie. As such, the theme was born!

To celebrate his weeknight first birthday, I decided to focus on a bright color palette and a few sweet details. Inspired by the Mustache Bash collection of paper goods by WH Hostess, the color combination of green, orange, teal and brown looks fresh and modern against the white décor of the party space. By focusing on a couple key ideas, I was able to make the space look festive without too much time or money. From a do-it-yourself banner, to a unique napkin fold for the dinner table, this party focuses on the man of the hour—the birthday boy!

After dinner, present your guests with one table styled with charming sweets for dessert. Keep it simple with a little candy, some dressed-up milk bottles and a smash cake for your sweet baby. A mustache and bow tie garland soars above to make the party space very festive.

Candy Jars

Create mini bow ties to wrap around candy jars or centerpiece vases. I used ¹/₂" yard (0.5m) of gingham fabric from my local craft store to create these cuties. It's a great way to add some personality to your display with minimal effort and expense. Follow the napkin folding instruction on the next page to create these bow tie embellishments.

Milk Bottles

Plastic milk bottles are the perfect addition to any kids' party. You don't need to worry about them breaking, and you can have them filled and chilled in the refrigerator ahead of time, leaving your hands free from pouring drinks during the party. To dress them up, we added cute striped straws and attached paper mustaches (found in the Templates section) with double-sided tape. That's a whole lot of style for very little effort!

Cookie Party Favors

Stick with your theme and send your guests home with a package of brightly frosted mustache cookies. Package them in a clear cellophane bag, and dress them up with a person-alized label. Create the label design in a computer design program and print them at home using label paper, or photocopy the label provided in the Templates section onto label paper.

FOLDED BOW TIE NAPKIN

Create a celebratory dinner table with one simple décor idea: a napkin folded in the shape of a bow tie! So simple to do, this is sure to delight your guests.

SUPPLIES

cloth napkins or fabric cut in 20" (51cm) squares • a ribbon or 2"× 5" (5cm × 13cm) strip of fabric • safety pin

1 Starting with your napkin open, fold in half longways, then again longways.

2 With your napkin horizontal, fold in both ends to meet in the center.

3 Pinch together and wrap the center with the 2"× 5" (5cm × 13cm) strip of fabric or ribbon and secure with a safety pin on the back.

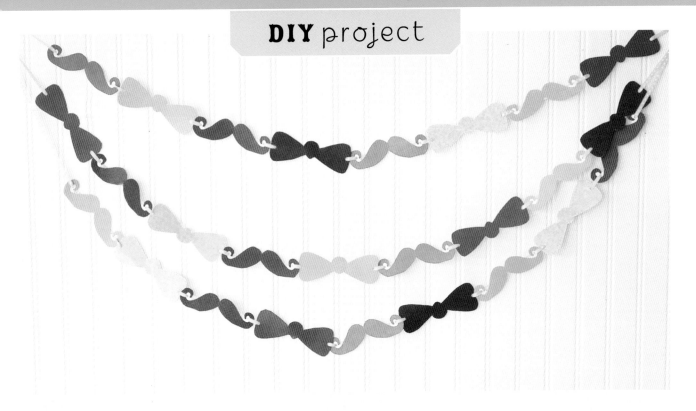

BOW TIE AND MUSTACHE GARLAND

◤ To execute the Little Man theme with a touch of preppy pizzazz, create a festive banner using theme-appropriate elements, such as mustaches and bow ties. This party décor is simple and easy to create. It can be used as a single strand, or double/triple them up for a more festive look!

SUPPLIES

color copies of the bow tie/mustache templates found in Templates section (Hint: Copy onto white cardstock or photo paper.) • scissors • hole punch • ribbon

1 Carefully using scissors, cut out the mustaches and bow ties. (Don't cut out the white area in the middle of the mustache end swirls; it's useful when punching holes for the ribbon!)

2 Once all of the items are cut out, punch a hole at each end of the shapes.

3 Weave your ribbon through the holes to attach your elements, alternating colors and shapes until you reach the desired length.

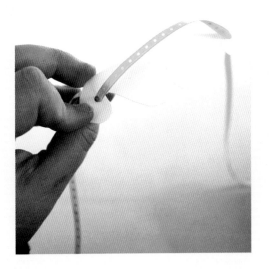

CAKE SMASH

A smash cake is one of the top party trends these days. Typically given to the birthday child at a first birthday celebration, it is meant to be smashed, smeared, enjoyed and consumed by the birthday boy or birthday girl. It's also a fabulous opportunity to get some great photographs of your baby celebrating this momentous occasion.

Gone are the days of serving a smashed cake to your party guests. Parties are serving up two cakes for the first birthday party: a smash cake for the guest of honor and the main decorated birthday cake (untouched by little hands) for the guests. The smash cake is typically a small, mini cake that coordinates with the party theme, but you could also use a cupcake or cake pop.

For a flawless cake smash, be prepared. Have a plan in place for location, props, photography and cleanup! Make sure you have everything already lined up before you allow baby to see the cake. Who is photographing? Is someone videotaping too? Make sure your camera batteries are charged and ready to go!

Clear the desired area of clutter and remove any distracting elements that you do not want in the background of your photos. Create a festive backdrop with balloons, ribbons or streamers. Let your child sit on the floor, instead of a high chair, so they have room to move and have fun!

Stick with white cake and white frosting. Stay away from chocolate cake (crumbles could look like dirt in photos) and red frosting (you don't want your baby to look like he/she is bleeding in photos!). Attract your baby's attention by adding some colorful decorations such as sprinkles or frosting polka dots in soft colors.

Dress your child in simple clothing that can get dirty. Bare feet are best, so you don't see dirty soles in your photographs.

Don't be discouraged if your child is timid and not flashing you picture-perfect smiles right out of the gate. He or she may be too curious or shy to pay attention to you at first. Give the baby a chance to discover the cake, and use that opportunity to take detail photos, such as capturing the hand just as he grabs a handful of the frosting. If all else fails, put a dollop of icing on their nose!

Take some photos with plenty of negative space at either the top, bottom or side. Those shots would be perfect with a little added text (via computer design software) to create a one-of-a-kind thank you note for your guests.

COOKIE PHOTO PROPS

Create a fun photo op with the birthday boy by serving up cookie props for guests to pose with. Bold-colored cookies in the shape of mustaches, bow ties and neckties make for a fun and silly addition to the party

SUPPLIES

premade sugar cookie dough · cookie cutters in desired shapes · lollipop sticks · piping bag and tip (for each color icing) · Royal icing (recipe below)

Royal Icing Recipe

1 cup (150g) confectioner's sugar

1 pasteurized egg white

$\frac{1}{4}$ tsp. vanilla extract

food coloring (as needed)

DIRECTIONS

Combine the above ingredients in the bowl of an electric mixer and whisk until thick. Add food coloring for desired colors.

Cookie Props Assembly

DIRECTIONS

Roll out store-bought sugar cookie dough and cut out shapes using desired cookie cutters. Insert a lollipop stick into the bottom of the cookie and place on a baking sheet. Bake according to instructions on the packaging, and let cool completely after removing them from the oven.

Fill your piping bag with royal icing (recipe above) and decorate the cookies as desired. Let dry completely before use.

resources

Invitation, paper goods, Cake Plate Clings (whhostess.com); fabric for bow tie napkins and décor (joanns.com), ribbon, clear cellophane bags for party favors, lollipop sticks for cookie props (michaels.com, joanns.com, hobbylobby.com); white textured tablecloth (fabric from dwellstudio.com); white dishes, silverware (crateandbarrel.com); plastic milk bottles, straws (shopsweetlulu.com); acrylic candy jars (containerstore.com); 6" (15cm) milk glass cake stand (shopsweetlulu.com).

5

MODERN SILHOUETTE

birthday party

MOST KIDS' PARTIES are planned around a theme: a princess, trains, a beloved character. For this party, I decided to think outside the box to create a stunning girl's birthday party sans the traditional princess theme. Here you will find ideas for a preppy silhouette themed party in a fresh green, black and white color palette with a fun pop of hot pink—a stylish party for any fair maiden.

The important elements for re-creating this event include a whimsical table setting, a delicious dessert table with color-coordinated sweets, and a fashionable DIY project that will make each guest party ready.

SETTING *the* THEME

The quickest way to make your party theme more unique is to add personalized elements: your daughter's name, age, monogram or even custom silhouette. Use the DIY instructions in this chapter to create your child's silhouette and add it to your party décor for a look that is all your own.

I love creating table settings for children that incorporate adult elements. For this party, I suggest setting up a series of child-size tables in a tea party-style.

Take Your Seat in Style

Guests young and old love to see their name on something pretty! Whether it's an escort card, a small gift or a hanging tag, dress up your guests' seats in style for your party.

For this event, I love the idea of hanging personalized plaques on ribbon on the back of each chair.

Personalized Décor

A party instantly becomes more personal and extra special when you personalize it! Add the birthday girl's name to some of the decorations, like a banner, cupcake toppers or door signage.

I enhanced our wheat grass and hot pink floral centerpieces with a custom centerpiece stick featuring the birthday girl's name and silhouette (found in Templates section).

Accessorize the Basics

Every table needs the basics: plates, silverware, napkins and glasses. Add a punch of color to accessorize your party table!

Color-coordinate your glasses, add some rickrack to your cloth napkins, and use colorful elements for your centerpieces, such as wheat grass plants or flowers.

SILHOUETTE

The décor of this party is focused around a modern spin on the traditional silhouette. Here are simple steps for you to follow in order to create your own. Once completed, you can use your silhouette on centerpiece sticks, chair nametags, cupcake toppers and signage.

SUPPLIES

profile photo of the guest of honor • small scissors • pencil • black paper or cardstock

1 From the photograph, carefully cut around the child's head, taking extra caution around the facial details.

2 With a pencil, trace the cutout template onto black paper.

3 Carefully cut out the silhouette, taking extra caution around the facial details. Apply to party décor for a fashionable and personalized look.

Although I suggest using black paper in the above instructions, you could adjust paper colors depending on your party décor. Contrast is important, as seen in the cannister embellishments.

PARTY HATS

Your little fashionistas will love dressing up with couture party hats for this festive fete. Using basic materials found at your local craft store and five simple steps, you can create a unique assortment of color-coordinated party hats.

SUPPLIES

paper hat template (found in the Templates section) · patterned paper · scissors · hot glue gun · ribbon and trim embellishments · elastic (optional)

1 Trace the template onto the back side of your selected paper, and cut out the shape.

2 Score the fold line. Bend and shape the template into the party hat cone shape.

3 Carefully place a line of glue along the seam and attach to the opposite side.

4 Gather up your embellishments. I suggest grosgrain ribbon, pompom trim, rickrack or tissue paper flowers. Glue on your choice of embellishment and allow to cool. (See the next page for some design ideas.)

5 Finish accessorizing your hat (I love a good bow!). If desired, add an elastic neck strap.

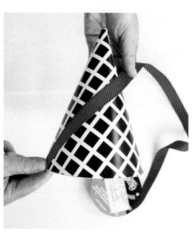

Party Hats with Style

Here are some ideas for embellishing your paper party hats:
Ribbons are an excellent way to add a touch of whimsy to your paper
party hats. I love a well-placed bow! Place it at the top, or along a row
of ribbon. You can also add personality with tissue paper or silk flowers.

Serve Up Your Sweets

Pull your desserts off the buffet table and serve them on a tray lined with coordinating patterned paper. There is no need to purchase new serving dishes for every event. Pull out your basic white collection, and change the look with reusable Cake Plate Clings or disposable scrapbook paper. Craft paper or wrapping paper also work well and are offered in countless options, making it simple to customize your party each and every time.

You can also accessorize your trays with ribbon, rickrack or fabric. I encourage you to think outside of the box to create a unique display for every celebration.

Coordinate Your Birthday Sweets

Your desserts will take on a festive yet chic look when you carry your color palette and icons throughout cookies, cupcakes and candy. Color-coordinated and theme-appropriate candy is a simple way to carry out your theme. For a princess party, crown lollipops would be ideal. For a nautical party, white lifesavers could take on the appearance of life preservers. For this party, a variety of green candies make our table look fresh and modern. Gummies, mints, gumballs and other candies were used as decoration.

Take your display a step further by labeling your sweets with coordinating tags and food tent cards. Simple accessories such as these will give your table a bespoke feel.

Create a well-balanced spread of desserts and candy using all white serving pieces. Dress them up with tray liners made out of coordinating paper or Cake Plate Clings (decorative, reusable liners).

Dress Up Your Cupcakes

Every birthday girl loves cupcakes—especially pretty ones! I dressed up store-bought cupcakes with custom fondant toppers. Initials are a great way to personalize cupcakes for each guest and tie in to this personalized theme perfectly.

There are many fondant designers in the marketplace whom you can work with to design custom toppers that coordinate with your color palette, patterns and silhouette perfectly. You can also craft your own using precolored fondant and cookie cutters, both readily available at your local craft store.

SASSY STRIPED MINI ICE CREAM CAKES

Wow your little lady and her guests with charming mini ice cream cakes. Try personalizing each one with her guests' initials or monogram.

INGREDIENTS (PER CAKE)

1 cup (240mL) vanilla ice cream

1 cup (240mL) chocolate sauce

2 medium-sized sugar cookies

2 tbsp. (30g) butter, melted

butter for greasing

gel piping pen

DIRECTIONS:

Grease a mini springform pan with a light coat of butter. Crumble up your sugar cookies and with a fork mix in the melted butter. Push the cookie mixture into the bottom of your springform pan to create the crust. Pour a fourth of your chocolate sauce on top of the cookie crust, and place in the freezer to harden for 5–10 minutes. Top with a fourth of the vanilla ice cream, smoothing it with a rubber spatula. Place back in the freezer for 5–10 minutes. Repeat this layering process until you reach the top of your pan. Once all of your layers are assembled, leave in the freezer until ready to serve. Once you remove the springform pans, use a gel piping pen to embellish the mini ice cream cakes with an initial or monogram.

resources

Photography by Kelly Lyden and Sisterazzi

Paper goods (whhostess.com); white table and chairs set, white pots, black plates (ikea.com); tablecloth made with white denim, black Swiss dot fabric and green piping trim (joanns.com); green glasses, child's silverware (potterybarnkids.com); wheat grass plants (wholefoods.com); green lollipops and candy (candywarehouse.com); green ribbon, black and white pompoms for garland, rickrack, ribbons (michaels.com, joanns.com or hobby-lobby.com); girl's pink dress (bodenusa.com); black striped hair bow (MelBelles via etsy.com); black console (potterybarn.com); glass candy jars (crateandbarrel.com, potterybarn.com); fondant cupcake toppers (Two Sugar Babies via etsy.com); white cake stand (tiffany.com).

CLASSIC NAUTICAL

birthday party

THERE ARE A FEW PARTY THEMES that are perfectly classic and timeless, and will remain current forever. A nautical theme is just that. It works for a girl, a boy, for a first birthday or a fourth birthday—it could even be darling for a baby shower! What's not to love about nautical stripes and preppy sailboats?

Classic elements such as an anchor, a sailboat and nautical flags are a simple addition to party décor. The theme lends itself to preppy patterns and a crisp color palette of navy blue, red and yellow, but you could reinvent any of the ideas in this chapter in a variety of modern color palettes (aqua and orange, pink and navy blue). This chapter will give you simple ideas to carry out the nautical theme, including some DIY décor projects, printable templates and a creative spin on a classic dessert recipe.

SETTING *the* THEME

Planning an event for children gives you the opportunity to create an experience—one that your guests will never forget! For a classic maritime theme, infuse nautical accents from start to finish. Tie a white rope around your striped party invitations, encourage your guests to play dress up with sailor hats and serve desserts that are not only delicious, but also fun to play with!

When planning your event, I encourage you to lay out your party ideas, and then take a step back. Try to view each party element through the eyes of a four-year-old to ensure that your child and his/her friends will have an absolutely amazing time.

Ahoy! Invitations

Set the tone for your event with a preppy striped party invitation. I have provided you with the template for this invitation and anchor tag (found in the Templates section) so you can easily fill in your customized information and send them to your guests. I attached the anchor cutout to the invitation with some white rope, which was purchased at my local hardware store.

Setting the Space

Décor for this theme includes a nautical flag banner, festive paper fans in red, white and blue, and paper lantern "buoys." I suggest focusing your décor and themed treats to the child's age and height level. For example, instead of setting up a formal table, set up a lower table that the children can walk right up to and grab their treat or a milk bottle.

A few throw pillows on the floor will create a comfy environment for kids to sit down and enjoy a treat, or get comfortable to float some sailboats and race them against their buddies.

Dress Up

Kids between the ages of three and five absolutely love to play dress up. Something as simple as a sailor hat can put them in the mood for a fabulous "day at sea" and make the party feel festive. For a personalized touch, have each child's name embroidered on the brim of the hat at your local monogram store. The hats will make for a darling party favor!

NAUTICAL MARITIME FLAGS

▚ Maritime flags are used to send signals to yachtsmen, each design representing a letter of the alphabet. The color blocking and preppy stripes are very festive and when strung together as a banner, make for a great party decoration!

SUPPLIES

nautical flag copies (templates found in the Templates section) • scissors • hole punch • white rope

1 Photocopy the nautical flag templates as many times as desired.

2 Carefully use scissors to cut out the photocopied nautical flags.

3 Punch two holes in the top of each flag, spaced about 2" (5cm) apart.

4 After laying out the flags in your desired order, string them onto white rope to create a banner or garland.

BUOY PAPER LANTERNS

SUPPLIES

12" (31cm) cylinder white paper lanterns · white rope · acrylic paint · paintbrushes · painter's tape

1 Assemble the paper lanterns according to the manufacturer's instructions.

2 Apply painter's tape to block off areas for color blocking or stripes.

3 Paint a coat of each color onto the paper lanterns. Repeat until you get the desired saturation of color.

4 Once the paint is dry, remove the painter's tape and clean up any rough edges with your paintbrush.

5 Hang several lanterns with white rope in a cluster, or spaced apart as a garland.

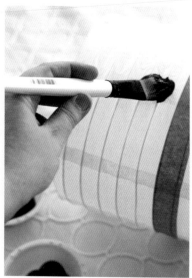

Napkin Rolls

Add a touch of nautical spirit to your silverware and napkins. Pairing polka dot or striped napkins with contrasting silverware is a great way to incorporate your color palette. Instead of tying the rolls with ribbon, use twine and embellish it with a white lifesaver to look like a life preserver.

Rope Embellishment

White rope can be used throughout the party as a consistent element. From embellishing the party invitations, to stringing the nautical flags, to wrapping it around vases for centerpieces, using it as a repeatable prop will assist you in styling a cohesive party.

◢ Dapper Party Favors

Party favor packaging is a fabulous way to send a little piece of your theme home with your guests. Continue the preppy nautical look into your packaging by using red and white striped paper bags tied with white rope and a navy "thank you" tag (found in the Templates section). Fill with a selection of nautical cookies, a paint-your-own sailboat kit or bathtub toys.

Sail Away

All kids have a fascination with water play. Create a water station using large containers or kid's pools where they can float and race boats. You can also float a fleet of small sailboats, each with a different number on the bottom. Have a prize associated with each number, so the child gets a surprise when they select a boat.

Sail Centerpiece
To create a sailboat centerpiece for my table, I wrapped a vase with white rope, filled it with Styrofoam and then topped it with candy. The sail was crafted out of two wood dowels (held together with rope), and a triangle of fabric. It was incredibly simple to put together and was a big hit with the children.

Sea Creatures

The nautical party theme lends itself to the inclusion of fish, bubbles, crabs and lobsters, as well as other nautical elements. In keeping with the color palette, I used red lobster lollipops as a special treat for the kids. Give any type of lollipops a special treatment by standing them upright in a container. Fill the container with Styrofoam, and then cover the top with candy so your lollipops stand upright.

Sailor's Sip

Little party guests get thirsty, so serve them up some refreshing milk in plastic bottles. No glass, easy to hold and even easier to dress up with a sticker, striped paper straw or twine and ribbon.

Striped Cookies

Sugar cookies are a fabulous vessel for executing a theme. They can be made in just about any shape and color combination, so you can truly design something unique to your party. One of my favorite options is to serve cookies in the number of the birthday child's age, or initial of their name. For this party, red and white striped "#4" cookies were the perfect addition to our nautical spread.

SAILBOAT RICE CEREAL TREATS

Turn a classic treat into something spectacular for your nautical party! This delicious rice cereal treats recipe can work for any occasion, but becomes seaworthy with the addition of colorful "sails."

Rice Cereal Treats

INGREDIENTS

3 tbsp. butter or margarine

4 cups (200g) miniature marshmallows

6 cups (156g) of rice cereal

DIRECTIONS

In a large saucepan, melt the butter over low heat. Slowly add in the miniature marshmallows and stir until completely melted. Remove from the heat and continue to stir. Slowly add in the rice cereal until all pieces are coated in the mixture.

Grease a 9"x 13" (23cm x 33cm) pan with cooking spray, and using a greased spatula, evenly press the mixture into the pan. Let it cool completely.

Sailboat Instructions

SUPPLIES

sail templates (found in Templates section) • 6" (15cm) white lollipop sticks • mini hole punch • rice cereal treats • oval cookie cutter • chocolate melts • piping bag and tip

DIRECTIONS

Once you have created your pan of rice cereal treats, use a greased oval cookie cutter to cut out your boat bases.

To decorate the bases, fill a piping bag with melted chocolate in your choice of color and carefully pipe on stripes, polka dots or even just a basic outline of the shape. Allow chocolate to harden before inserting the sails.

To craft the sails, photocopy the sail templates (found in the Templates section) as many times as needed. Carefully cut out the sails. Using a small hole punch, place a hole at both the top and bottom of the sail, trying to line them up as evenly as possible. Starting with the front of the sail, insert a white lollipop stick through both holes, allowing the sail to bow forward slightly. Insert the sail into the center of a rice cereal treat.

resources

Paper goods, Cake Plate Clings (whhostess.com); low table (crateandbarrel.com); wood dowels for sail, paint and brushes for buoys (michaels.com); navy fabric for sail (joanns.com); child sailor hat (amazon.com); galvanized buckets (ikea.com); patterned paper fans (partycity.com); white rope (homedepot.com); white cylinder paper lanterns (paperlantern-store.com); square plastic milk bottles, red striped bags, polka dot napkins, red paper plates (shopsweetlulu.com); wood sailboats (amazon.com); striped "4" cookies (fireflyconfections.com); red lobster lollipops (candywarehouse.com).

7

FORMAL TEA

birthday party

TEA PARTIES ARE A RITE OF PASSAGE for little girls. They get to dress up, pretend to be a grown-up and pour tea for their friends, serve up cookies and sweets, and revel in playing hostess for the first time.

Sweet and girly, I am going to share ideas with you to create a perfect afternoon for your favorite little ones. From simple DIY décor projects, to a unique way to serve up my go-to vanilla cupcakes, this party is full of sweet details that will leave your little girl and her friends feeling extra fancy!

Chair Décor

Add a pop of pink to your basic white tea table with the addition of oversized bows on the chair backs. I found 4" (10cm) wide ribbon at my local craft store, and wrapped the trim around the chair back and tied it in a bow. It is a quick addition to your party décor, but will make a big impact.

Accessorizing the Table

Top the table with a sheer tablecloth with a touch of shimmer, a tea tin centerpiece, a silver tea set and mini teacups ready for pouring. Although toy tea cups are quite fun, grown-up tea cups are even more special. Search out your local thrift stores, resale shops or garage sales for "vintage" tea cups and saucers to use for the party.

Fascinators

Getting dressed up for a party is half the fun—putting on your prettiest party dress, polished Mary Janes, and of course, an accessory or two. Take a cue from the fashionable Brits and try replacing your hair bow with a fascinator headband. The poof of fur or feathers adds some height and drama and looks downright charming on a little girl.

Doily Garland

Repeat the use of doilies throughout your whole party, from the invitation to DIY doily garlands. Using white paper doilies in varying sizes, I made these garlands by simply folding the doily in half and attaching it around a piece of yarn with glue dots.

DOILY PARTY INVITATIONS

Adding a doily border and ribbon embellishment to your party invitation adds a touch of "fancy" that every little girl will love. The doily accessory can be repeated throughout the party to create a cohesive look.

SUPPLIES

8" (20cm) round white doilies • 5" (13cm) circle invitation template (found in the Templates section) • hole punch • ¼" (6mm) thick ribbon • double-stick tape or glue dots

1 Photocopy the circle invitation template (found in the Templates section) as many times as needed.

2 Cut out each circle template and handwrite your information (or use a computer program to print on them).

3 Attach a circle template to the center of a doily using double-stick tape or glue dots.

4 Using a hole punch, place two holes about 1" (3cm) apart at the top of the circle.

5 Weave a 6" (15cm) piece of ¼" (6mm) thick ribbon through the two holes. Tie the ribbon into a bow.

love the idea of infusing décor props into a party space. This precious teacart was the perfect accessory for my fancy tea party, and it held all of the desserts. This would make a darling present for the birthday girl, providing hours of fun after the party is over.

Heart Mini Cake

I often choose one or two icons to use in design elements for a party. For this particular one, a sweet pink heart seemed like the perfect fit. I served up a variety of pink sweets at my fancy tea party, including this darling 5" (13cm) round pink cake that was embellished with a frosting heart.

Pink Candy

Small bowls of pink candy are the perfect accessory to our dessert cart. Wrapped hard candy, pink chocolate candies, rock candy sticks and swirl lollipops are some of my favorite options.

Heart Cookies

I continued my use of heart details throughout the party by having one of my favorite cookie designers create miniature heart sugar cookies. Covered in pale pink edible glitter, they added the perfect amount of shimmer to our dessert table.

Dance Party

A dance party is the perfect time to introduce another fun element—ribbon wands—into your party (instructions for this DIY project found on next page). A little free dance will get your guests grooving to the music and have a blast with their new toy.

RIBBON WANDS

Little girls love to pretend to be princesses. So whether you are hosting a princess-themed tea party or just a fancy-schmancy tea party, ribbon wands are a great accessory that will make your little guests feel like royalty.

SUPPLIES

12" (31cm) strips of ribbon (varying widths and colors) • 11" (28cm) white lollipop sticks • small jingle bells • decorative thumbtacks • hot glue gun

1 Take three 12" (31cm) pieces of ribbon and lay them atop one another. At one end, place a dab of hot glue between each of the three ribbons to adhere them together.

2 Attach a small jingle bell to a 3" (8cm) piece of narrow ribbon. Using a decorative thumbtack, attach the ribbon to the very top of a white lollipop stick. You can either cut the ends off the ribbon, or glue them down with a glue gun.

3 Using your hot glue gun, attach the cluster of three ribbons to the top inch of the white lollipop stick. Once the glue hardens, wrap the ribbons around the stick just slightly and apply more hot glue to hold them in place.

RIBBON CHANDELIER

Chandeliers make any room special, so of course they would have the same impact on a party! My ribbon chandeliers are simple to construct and can be created in any size, with any color combination, making it very versatile party décor. And after you delight your guests with this creation at the party, you can repurpose the chandelier in your child's bedroom or playroom.

SUPPLIES

wood insert of an embroidery hoop • ribbon • hot glue gun • scissors

1 Cut your ribbon into 18"–20" (46cm–51cm) strips.

2 Fold each ribbon in half. Wrap around the wood hoop, pulling the ends through the bent loop to create a "knot."

3 Before pulling the "knot" taut, insert a dot of hot glue between the outside of the wood hoop and the ribbon. Pull the ribbon to create a tight bond.

4 Repeat around the entire hoop. You can alternate ribbon colors or textures to create a pattern, or do a varied assortment for a more random design.

5 After you have completely surrounded the hoop with ribbon, attach two pieces of ribbon to the inside edges, crisscrossing them to create a balanced hanging device. This length should be adjusted to your desired hanging location.

6 Trim up any ribbon ends that may be too long, and then your ribbon chandelier is ready to be hung.

TEACUP CUPCAKE RECIPE

A delicious vanilla cupcake will be that much sweeter when served in a pretty teacup with a shimmering heart cupcake topper.

Cream Cheese Frosting

INGREDIENTS

16 oz. (450g) cream cheese, softened

½ cup (110g) butter, softened

2 cups (300g) confectioners' sugar, sifted

1 tsp. vanilla extract

DIRECTIONS

In the bowl of your stand mixer, cream together the cream cheese and butter until smooth. Add in the vanilla extract and then gradually stir in the confectioners' sugar. Chill in the refrigerator until ready to pipe onto your cupcakes.

Cake Recipe

INGREDIENTS

1 stick (110g) butter, softened

2 eggs

$^2/_3$ cup (177mL) milk

1 cup (225mL) white granulated sugar

1$^1/_2$ tsp. vanilla extract

1$^1/_2$ cups (165g) all-purpose flour

$^1/_2$ tsp. baking powder

$^1/_2$ tsp. salt

DIRECTIONS

Preheat oven to 350°F (180°C or gas mark 4). Line your muffin pans with cupcake liners. (This recipe will yield 12 cupcakes.)

In a medium-sized bowl, cream together the butter and sugar. Add the eggs one at a time, continuing to beat after each addition. Once combined, stir in the vanilla extract.

In a separate bowl, mix together the dry ingredients. Slowly sift the dry ingredients into the butter mixture, and then add the milk. Evenly distribute the batter among the cupcake liners, filling each one approximately two-thirds full.

Bake for 20–24 minutes.

Tea Cup Party Favors

Remember earlier when I suggested searching your local thrift stores for teacups and saucers? Consider sourcing enough of them to use as party favors, too! Place the teacup and saucer into a cellophane bag and fill the cup with candy or small trinkets. Tie the bag up with ribbon and attach a sweet polka dotted thank you tag (found in the Templates section) thanking your guests for coming.

resources

White table and chairs (ikea.com); white tea cart, silver tea set (potterybarnkids.com); ribbon chandelier supplies, doilies, ribbon wand supplies (michaels.com, hobbylobby.com or joanns.com); 4" (10cm) wide pink ribbon for chair décor (joanns.com); miniature heart cake (marianos.com); pink candy and lollipops (candywarehouse.com); shimmer heart cookies (fireflyconfections.com); blah blah doll (landofnod. com), pink striped napkins (shopsweetlulu.com); girls' fascinators (etsy.com/shop/cocorosecouture).

8

BARNYARD BASH

birthday party

A BARNYARD BIRTHDAY BASH IS PERFECT for toddler to elementary school-aged children. With a few creative details and an afternoon spent down on the farm, it's the perfect combination of "experience" and "party" that I always strive to provide at my events.

There are a few classic staples that every barnyard party must have: red gingham check, hay and animals! In this chapter, I will share my ideas for styling a party that has modern details, but is classic at heart, leaving all of your guests ready to party 'til the cows come home!

SETTING *the* THEME

A combination of fabulous patterns including polka dots, a barnyard gingham and colorful leaves in a fresh color palette of aqua blue, red and a dash of yellow and green will make your barnyard bash the talk of the farm. Infuse your party with these cute yet mod ideas to create the perfect event for your little party animal.

When planning a party at an outside location, focus your efforts on just one main table. For this party, I styled a festive snack table that held all of the themed elements to create a look that would delight the children. I also had hats and bandanas readily available for dress-up, darling animal feed bags for the petting zoo and a few themed activities in my back pocket.

Dress the Part
Kids at this age love to dress up! Encourage creativity and imagination by providing them with props for their day on the farm. Straw cowboy hats and bandannas are the perfect accessories.

Inspiring Invitations
The color palette and details of this party were inspired by the Barnyard Farm Animals party invitation from WH Hostess. The modern animal silhouettes and fresh color palette of red, aqua blue, green and yellow are playful for kids, yet appeal to the parents as well. The elements from this collection are repeated throughout the party, helping to create a cohesive look.

◣ Activity
A barnyard theme lends itself to an ideal activity for kids of all ages—a petting zoo! Look for a local company that will travel with their animals to your home. The children will love seeing and touching the chicks, baby goats and maybe even ride horses! Provide your guests with muslin bags full of animal feed dressed up with my custom iron-on transfer (found in the Templates section).

ANIMAL FEED BAGS

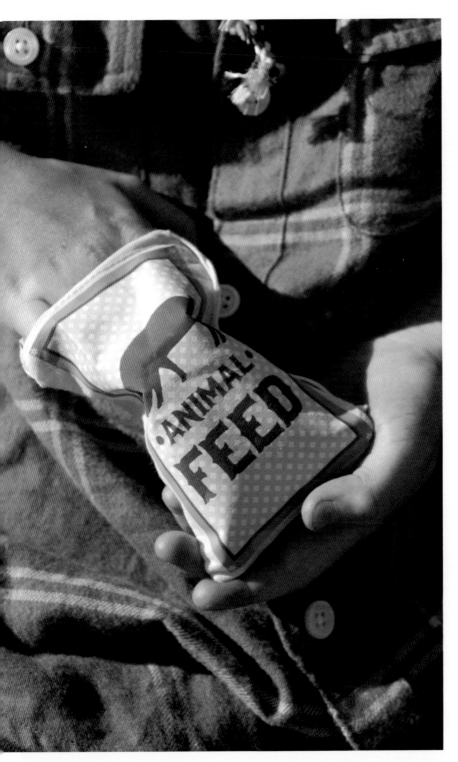

■ Since the highlight of the barnyard bash is petting the animals, it seems only appropriate that you have fabulous feedbags to hand out to each of your guests. This project is VERY simple:

SUPPLIES

3" × 5" (8cm × 13cm) muslin bags • iron-on transfer paper • iron • scissors • animal feed template (found in the Templates section)

1 Take the animal feed printable template to your local print shop along with iron-on transfer paper (available at your local craft shop). Copy the template onto the transfer paper, one copy for each guest.

2 Cut out the individual tags and iron onto the muslin bags following the instructions on the paper.

3 Allow the bags to cool completely before handling and filling with animal feed.

DESSERTS DETAILS

Whether you are hosting your party at home or on an actual farm, setting up one long table for your farm hands (or guests) to eat at is ideal. A classic, red gingham tablecloth will assist you in setting the tone for a family-friendly picnic. Oftentimes, an outdoor table can be dressed to the nines and still look lost in a big, open space. One way to add a punch of color and create some height interest is with the use of balloons. Take a modern approach and use single 36" (91cm) balloons instead of a traditional cluster. Depending on the length of your table, I would suggest two or three balloons spaced out as necessary.

Setting the Table

Rustic galvanized containers can be repurposed for this party as centerpieces or to present snack mix to hungry farm hands. Instead of filling the centerpiece containers with flowers, I took a more natural approach and used popcorn—another fun treat for guests to munch on. A personalized center-piece stick added a pop of color and helped celebrate the birthday child.

Treats for the Party Animals

All party animals need a snack at some point! After an afternoon of petting animals, going on hay rides and getting lost in corn mazes, I served up fresh, farmhouse milk in plastic milk bottles with striped straws, cute animal-shaped cookies and homemade strawberry shortcake in individual Mason jars. Wooden spoons were tied to the Mason jars with twine for easy serving.

Break Time

Working (or playing) on a farm all day is hard work, so encourage the kids to sit down and relax for a bit while enjoying their snacks. This is a great opportunity to have the birthday child open his/her gifts, read a theme-appropriate book, or prepare your next activity.

PARTY FAVOR JARS

If you are looking for a unique way to present party favors, I have just the project for you. This idea could be reinterpreted for so many different themes and holidays, as well as any color palette!

SUPPLIES

small jars with lids • small plastic toy animals • spray paint primer • spray paint in desired color • hot glue gun

1 Remove the lids from the jars. Working over a drop cloth, spray each lid and plastic animal with a coat of primer and let dry fully. Repeat if necessary.

2 Using a hot glue gun, carefully apply dots of glue on the feet of your primed animals, and attach to the top of the primed jar lids. Allow glue to set fully.

3 Spray the lids with your desired color of spray paint. It may take a few coats to fully cover. Allow to dry completely.

4 Once the lids are completely dry, you can fill the jars. I suggest placing some green shredded paper in the bottom of the jar to look like grass. You can add animal crackers, candy or small toys.

Hint: Spray-painting the lids two different colors can offer a festive look to your party favor display. You can also personalize each jar with your guests' names using a paint pen.

STRAWBERRY SHORTCAKE

I love the idea of incorporating mason jars into this party. They have an old-fashioned feel to them, and serving up individual desserts makes for less hands-on time for the host—no need to stand and cut the cake!

INGREDIENTS AND SUPPLIES

white cake mix

2" (5cm) circular cookie cutter

whipped cream

strawberries

sugar

pastry bag with large star tip

mason jars

wooden spoons

twine

INSTRUCTIONS

Prepare the cake mix as instructed, baking it in a full sheet pan. Allow the cake to cool completely, and then using a 2" (5cm) circular cookie cutter, cut out as many rounds as possible. Place aside for assembling.

Rinse, hull and slice your strawberries. Sprinkle heavily with granulated sugar and stir to combine. Cover and place in a refrigerator for at least 30 minutes.

Fill a large pastry bag fitted with a large star tip with whipped cream and set aside.

ASSEMBLY

Gather your cake rounds, strawberries and piping bag full of whipped cream, as well as your mason jars, wooden spoons and twine.

In your freshly washed mason jar, place a round of cake in the bottom, followed by two scoops of strawberries (and juice), topped off with a piped circle of whipped cream. Repeat these layers until the jar is full. If serving immediately, no need for a top. If you are transporting these to a party location, the jar tops make these ideal for packing in a cooler on ice.

Prior to serving, I like to style the jars with spoons ready for eating. Use twine to loop around the jar and hold a wooden spoon in place.

ACTIVITY 💡 IDEAS

Hayride

As a child, what could be better than a hayride on a sunny afternoon with all of your friends? It doesn't get much better than that! A hayride is a great activity for kids, and since they have to remain seated for the duration of the ride, it is also an opportunity to encourage them to partake in a couple of theme-related activities such as:

Sing-alongs

Encourage kids to sing along to some animal- or barnyard-related songs that they have learned at school over the years like "Farmer in the Dell," "B-I-N-G-O," "Old MacDonald had a Farm" or "Ba-Ba-Black Sheep."

Circle Games

Sitting in the hay is a great setup for circle games! A round of hot potato or duck duck goose would be fun. You can also encourage kids to look around their surroundings and play a group game of I spy.

Photo Ops

It's always important to be prepared for that perfect photo op during your party. So much work goes into planning, you want to ensure that you will have lasting photos to remember the day. I suggest bringing along a few items in your camera bag to pull out when the occasion arises. My suggestions include: a pennant banner, ribbon wands or flags for kids to fly.

A hayride is certainly an ideal photo op! You will have all of the kids in one place and they will be eager to pose on such a fun ride. I suggest taking a few extra photos with lots of negative space on one side of the main focal point. After the party, you can add some text to your photo with the aid of computer design software, and use it as your thank you note. It will be a fabulous reminder of your barnyard bash.

Buried Treasure Games

When the hay ride is not in motion, play a round of hidden treasure. Prior to boarding the truck, make arrangements with the driver to hide items under the hay for the kids to find. Small items such as plastic toy animals all the way up to larger items like hula hoops will delight the kids as they toss the hay around searching.

resources

Invitation, centerpiece sticks, banner (whhostess.com); straw cowboy hats, bandannas (orientaltrading.com); galvanized tub containers (ikea.com); square plastic milk bottles, striped straws, 36" (91cm) balloons, wooden spoons, red twine (shopsweetlulu.com); mini mason jars (walmart.com); muslin feed bags, iron-on transfer paper, spray paint, primer, mini plastic animal toys, hot glue gun (michaels.com, joanns.com, hobbylobby.com); party favor jars (containerstore.com); cookies (Cookies on the Side by Pam DeGuzman).

9

FIESTA!

birthday party

FROM BOLD FLAVORS TO BRIGHT COLORS, a fiesta-themed party is a unique party your child will love. String up Mexican papel picado banners and flags, serve fruity punches with colorful straws and set up a make-your-own taco bar for lunch. This theme is fabulous for slightly older children who can participate in games such as Pass the Sombrero or limbo under the Mexican banners.

The bright color palette of hot pink, orange, yellow and lime green looks very playful in this party with the combination of colorful chevron and polka dot patterns. Read on to learn how to throw a celebratory fiesta full of sweet details.

SETTING *the* THEME

Infuse the warm colors of Mexico into your party décor with colorful papel picado banners, tissue paper fringe accessories and a festive table setting that will delight your guests.

Set up a low table with floor pillows instead of chairs. Dress the table with a textured tablecloth, colorful plates and napkins and unique DIY centerpieces including yarn poof flowers, and fringe centerpiece sticks.

Mexican Party Banner
Papel picado ("perforated paper") is a decorative craft made by cutting paper into elaborate designs. Known as a Mexican folk art, papel picado flags are used to create banners for celebrations and holiday decorations in many countries. Use these banners to hang above your party space to create a festive atmosphere.

Pass the Sombrero Game
Reinvent the classic hot potato party game that involves players gathering in a circle and tossing a small object such as a beanbag to each other while music plays. Instead of using a beanbag, use a theme-appropriate sombrero hat. Directions: The player who is holding the sombrero when the music stops is out. Play continues until only one player is left.

Confetti
Colorful paper confetti works into the Fiesta theme perfectly. It adds a festive touch to tabletops, and kids love to throw it in the air! Carry the confetti element throughout the party—starting with the invitation. Use it for décor, and incorporate an edible version by using colorful sprinkles on desserts.

CONFETTI PARTY INVITATION

Create a colorful party invitation to invite your guests to the fiesta using this festive invitation. The surprise in the envelope is that it is full of confetti, giving your guests a peek into the fun that is to come at the party.

SUPPLIES:

fiesta invitations (found in Templates section) • glassine envelopes (4¼" × 2½" [11cm × 6cm]) • colorful paper confetti • glue dots or double-stick tape

1 Photocopy the fiesta invitation template (found in the Templates section) as many times as needed.

2 Cut out each invitation and handwrite your information (or use a computer program to print on them).

3 Fill each glassine bag with a handful of colorful confetti.

4 Place glue dots or strips of double-stick tape onto the back (so the envelope flap is facing up), and attach to the center of your fiesta party invitation.

FRINGE CENTERPIECE STICK

Using a colorful fringe garland, create special centerpiece sticks to adorn your party tables. You can customize these with your child's age or initial, and to coordinate with any color palette.

SUPPLIES

tissue paper fringe garland • wood number or letter (6"–10" [15cm–25cm] tall) • 11" (28cm) white lollipop stick • hot glue gun

1 Glue a white lollipop stick to the back of a wood number or letter, placing it at least halfway up to create a balanced centerpiece stick.

2 Starting at one end, use a hot glue gun to place a dab of glue on the wood number or letter and attach the end of the fringe garland.

3 Once the glue is dry, start wrapping the garland around the number or letter. Occasionally place a dab of glue under it to hold in place.

4 Once you have wrapped your entire number or letter, glue the end of the fringe to secure it in place.

5 Use your scissors to carefully trim any interior holes or shapes to clearly define the number or letter.

6 Stick the number/letter into a centerpiece base, such as a small pot of grass.

YARN POOF FLOWERS

Forgo natural flower arrangements for this party and make
your own yarn poof flowers.
They will add a pop of color and
texture to your table décor, and
it's such a simple craft, your child
can assist you in construction.

SUPPLIES

color-coordinated yarn • 6" (15cm) white lollipop sticks • hot glue gun •
scissors

1 Wrap a single color of yarn around four of your fingers, continuing to go
round and round until you have a very thick bunch.

2 Weave the end of the yarn between your two middle fingers and wrap it
around the outside of your bunch.

3 Gently pull the bundle off your fingers and tie off the end, squeezing
the yarn tight around the center of your bundle.

4 Using scissors, cut through the loops on both sides. Fluff the individual
yarn ends to make a full ball.

5 Using your hot glue gun, carefully apply a large dab of glue to the top
$^1/_2$" (13cm) of the white lollipop stick and attach the yarn poof to the top.
Hold the ball in place until the glue dries (just a minute or so).

6 Use scissors to trim the yarn poof so it is a nice round shape.

PARTY FAVOR PAPER CONES

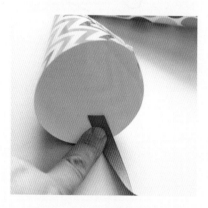

◤ Send your guests home with a party favor that reflects the style of the party: colorful and festive. Craft these darling paper cones using my templates or scrapbook paper, embellish them with ribbon or tissue paper fringe and then fill them with candy or small trinkets. They are also a great container to give to the guests if you plan to do a piñata—perfect for filling up with candy!

SUPPLIES

paper cone templates and gift tags (found in the Templates section) • tissue paper fringe garland • 12" (30cm) ribbon • scissors • hot glue gun • paper clips

1 Photocopy the paper cone templates and gift tags (found in the Templates section), making one of each for each guest. Cut out each paper cone template. Bend it to form the cone shape, and apply a paper clip at the top for easy maneuvering. Using a hot glue gun, apply a line of glue along the inside seam where the two ends meet. Press the other end on top of the glue and allow it to dry completely.

2 Using a dab of glue on the inside of your cone, attach a hanging ribbon. Repeat on the opposite side to create a handle.

3 Glue the tissue paper fringe garland around the top edge of the paper cone. Pom pom trim, ribbon or rickrack would also make a stylish embellishment.

4 Attach the coordinating gift tag to the side of the handle and fill with goodies.

Wooden Utensils

One of my new favorite trends in the party world is the decorated bamboo utensil. Available in a variety of colors, patterns and motifs, it's a great way to infuse your color palette onto your food table.

Sprinkle Ice Cream Cones

Carry the confetti element of your party décor into dessert! Colorful sprinkles mimic the look of confetti, so use them in volume for this party!

To create my sprinkle-dipped ice cream cones, simply dip the top $\frac{1}{2}$" (13cm) of the cone into melted chocolate and then immediately into a bowl full of sprinkles. Stand upright and allow the chocolate to harden before filling with ice cream.

resources

Multicolored and pink tissue paper fringe garland, paper straws, mason jar lids, wood spoons, acrylic ice cream cone holder (shopsweetlulu.com); paper goods, chevron plates, Cake Plate Clings (whhostess.com); fabric for tablecloth, cake stand pom pom trim (joanns.com); Mexican papel picado flag garland, glassine envelopes and confetti for invitations, colorful sprinkles (amazon.com); sombrero (orientaltrading.com); floor pillows (homegoods.com); white pots (ikea.com); grass plants (wholefoods.com; mason jars (walmart.com); wood number, 11" (28cm) lollipop sticks, 6" (15cm) lollipop sticks, yarn (michaels.com, joanns.com or hobbylobby.com); pink rock candy, striped hard candy (candywarehouse.com); "eat me" acrylic cake topper (etsy.com/shop/MissSarahCake); pink and yellow pettiskirts (shoptomkat.com).

Mason Jar Drinks

The mason jar (or canning jar) has become very popular as a party accessory in the last few years. It's a timeless item that has been repurposed for modern parties, mainly as centerpiece vessels or a creative way to hold drinks. For kids' parties, I suggest topping them with a cutout lid. It may hinder spills, and has the perfect spot to accessorize the drink with a patterned straw. For the fiesta theme, serve up colorful punches in them.

PAR | TEE

AT THE
WILL MILLER
GOLF CLASSIC

in honor of his 6th birthday

saturday, june 10, 2013 • 11am

MILLER GOLF & COUNTRY CLUB

rsvp to book your tee time!
millerclassic@gmail.com

10

GOLF CLASSIC

birthday party

CLASSIC BOY PARTY THEMES often include sports: baseball, tennis, soccer, football and very often, golf. A celebration centered on a sport offers you an instant party activity and is typically quite simple to plan. If your little man loves heading to the golf course, plan a preppy event full of themed details, crisp green grass, and a navy blue and white color palette.

This chapter shares ideas on how to infuse your party with design elements that will make your guests feel like they are celebrating on the eighteenth hole: a festive table setting with DIY décor ideas, a "putting green" dessert table and themed desserts.

SETTING *the* THEME

When it comes to boy parties, I am always careful to make sure the decorations weren't too cute. I prefer to focus on handsome designs—clean and preppy. Using crisp color palettes, I focus my attention on creating décor that will appeal to the guests. For this Golf Classic, that meant creating a festive table setting for lunchtime, a dessert table that would "wow" guests, and a fun game to keep them entertained.

I consistently used several design elements across the three focus areas to achieve a cohesive party design. Those elements included navy and white striped ribbon, galvanized containers, wheat grass and golf balls.

The ideas in this chapter are easily replicated for a party at home or at an outside location. If you are hosting your event at a local miniature golf course and only have one party table to decorate, no problem. Use these key items and ideas and create one amazing table that tells your story.

Water Holes
Golfers get thirsty! Provide water bottles for your guests and dress them up with water bottle labels (found in the Templates section).

Tee-Off Placecards
Get creative with your place settings; fill mini galvanized buckets with wheat grass, a golf tee and a personalized golf ball. Simply use a dab of hot glue to attach the ball and tee together for stability.

Themed Centerpieces
Infuse your theme into the center-pieces by filling vases with whiffle balls, and galvanized tubs with wheat grass and my découpage flags. Instructions are found on the next page.

DÉCOUPAGE FLAGS

Create your own flags with patterned paper and cardboard flags. To further customize your party décor, you can add your child's age onto the flags.

SUPPLIES:

cardboard flags • patterned paper • solid paper • découpage glue • sponge paintbrush • spray adhesive • craft knife

1 Spray adhesive onto the back side of the patterned paper, and place the cardboard flag onto the glue. Allow the glue to dry completely.

2 Carefully use a craft knife to cut out the flag from the paper. Repeat on the other side of the flag.

3 Cut out the number you would like on the flag from solid paper. Attach to the front of the flag with découpage glue.

4 Using a sponge brush, liberally apply découpage glue on top of the papered sides of the flag. Allow the flag to dry completely before repeating.

Bucket of Balls Party Favor

Send your little golfers home with their very own "bucket of balls." Fill a galvanized tub with a bag of whiffle balls and tees. Tie my gift tag that says, "Thanks for teeing off with me!" to the side of the bucket (found in the Templates section).

Golf Ball Wall Décor

Using a few basic items from the party store, create a decorative wall in your home that can serve as a backdrop to a party table or birthday photos. I used a white paper fan ball (only expanded halfway) and a "tee" cut out from blue poster board to create this wall display—the perfect place to "tee off" the party.

Ball Toss Game

Boys like to be active! Keep your guests occupied during the party with a simple ball toss game. Using galvanized containers, I wrapped them with coordinating ribbon and labeled them each with a different number. Whiffle balls are the "toss" of choice to ensure nothing gets broken when the balls start flying through the air. Provide a prize for the child that gets the ball in the most buckets.

DESSERTS *and* DETAILS

Styling a dessert table around the Golf Classic theme is a preppy hostess' dream come true. A classic color palette, the option to embellish basic desserts with themed accessories, and a clean layout that allows for color-coordinated branding with paper goods—what's not to like?

I designed this dessert table to look like it was sitting atop a putting green. Using a piece of indoor/outdoor carpet that I found at my local hardware store to line the tabletop, I covered the edges with a 4" (10cm) wide navy blue and white striped grosgrain ribbon.

To mimic the galvanized centerpieces and placecards on the lunch table, I used a three-tiered galvanized stand in the center of the table, as well as two containers holding wheat grass and my découpage flags. I wrapped navy and white striped ribbon around each tier of the three-tier stand, and topped it with a paper fan that I created out of coordinating paper. You could create the same look with any scrapbook or wrapping paper.

Desserts on the table included cupcakes with coordinating flag toppers, sugar cookies shaped like golf balls, powdered sugar donut "holes in one," chocolate-dipped pretzels (or "irons and woods") and polka dot cups full of candy.

Here are a few fun ideas to embellish the theme:

- Use a Lucite tray upside down as a riser, and line whiffle balls underneath it for a pop of the theme.

- Whether it's plastic or bamboo utensils, you can quickly embellish the handles with washi tape. Available in endless patterns and colors, it's a great way to carry out your theme.

- Brand your table with coordinated signage, including food tent cards, candy, jar tags and cupcake flags.

Golf Cupcakes

Top your basic vanilla cupcakes with green frosting and a darling flag topper. Using my templates (found in the Templates section), 4" (10cm) white lollipop sticks and glue dots, you can re-create these for your Golf Classic.

Cookies in Grass Plants

To create sugar cookies that look like golf balls, pipe tonal polka dots in an all-over pattern. Firefly Confections made these darling cookies for me, and baked them on white lollipop sticks, so I could stand them up in a pot of wheat grass. The food tent card is found in the Templates section.

Irons and Woods Pretzel Sticks

Chocolate-dipped pretzels are a favorite treat and offer a fun opportunity for themed signage, labeling them "Irons and Woods."

Donut Holes (in One)

Serve up a quick treat in between games: donut "Holes in One." I arranged powdered sugar donut holes in cupcake liners for easy serving.

GOLF CLUB-WICHES

Dress up a basic club sandwich with paper wrappers to make them party ready.

INGREDIENTS AND SUPPLIES

bread

sandwich makings

condiments

3"x 8" (8cm x 20cm) patterned paper

DIRECTIONS:

After assembling the ingredients you want on your sandwiches, stack them together and cut off the crusts so your sandwiches are a consistent size and shape. Wrap a piece of patterned paper around the back half of the sandwich.

resources

Paper goods, Cake Plate Clings (whhostess.com); green indoor/outdoor carpet (homedepot.com); golf balls and tees (target.com); large galvanized pots (ikea.com); mini galvanized pots, whiffle balls (amazon.com); bamboo utensils, navy blue stripe washi tape, blue polka dot and blue stripe cupcake liners (shopsweetlulu.com); 4" (10cm) wide navy and white stripe ribbon (joanns.com); three-tier galvanized container (potterybarn.com); wheat grass plants (wholefoods.com); blue chocolate melts for pretzels (michaels. com); cardboard flags, découpage glue (paper-source.com); white tray (williams-sonoma.com); golf ball cookies (fireflyconfections.com); white paper fan balls (partycity.com); navy blue poster board (michaels.com).

11

LOVE BUG SOIRÉE

valentine's day party

AFTER THE RUSH OF THE HOLIDAY SEASON dies down, February looms ahead as the gateway to spring. Even though it's a short month, with nothing to look forward to, it can often feel quite long. Valentine's Day is the perfect opportunity to surprise your kids with a Love Bug play date with their friends. Put a Valentine's Day spin on the classic ladybug party theme to allow spring details such as wheat grass and a bright green pop of color to look fresh during the cold winter month.

This chapter will help you create your own ladybug invitation, set a charming table full of themed details, bake the cutest cupcakes in town, and entertain your guests with playful games and activities.

SETTING *the* THEME

Set one fabulous table with different elements to tie together the theme: cover the table in a white and black polka dot tablecloth, top it with three wheat grass centerpieces featuring "love bug" centerpiece sticks, and identify each guest's place setting with a DIY felt place mat.

Balloon Love

Balloons make any event more festive! Source balloons that fit into both your theme and color palette at your local or online party stores. For Valentine's Day, a mixture of red and white is perfect, especially if they are heart-shaped.

Overhead party space can often be overlooked, placing the focus on the table setting. Balloons help define the vertical space around a table, so attach them to chairs or tie them to the four corners of the table to add decoration and define the party area.

◤ **Love Bug Centerpiece Sticks**

Centerpiece sticks are a fabulous way to add themed décor to any party. Use the centerpiece template (found in the Templates section) to create a set of your own. Simply photocopy and punch out the template using a 3" (8cm) circle punch and use glue dots to attach two of them together (backside to backside). Insert one 11" (28cm) white lollipop stick and embellish with a bow.

Felt Place Mats

Using red, black and white felt, create place mats that look like ladybugs. Use puffy paint to outline the heart "spots" and draw on eyes.

LOVE BUG PARTY INVITATION

◤ Young guests will delight in receiving this interactive party invitation. Follow the steps below to create your own lady bug invitations.

SUPPLIES

circle invitation template (found in the Templates section) • black scrapbook paper • 3" (8cm) circle hole punch • red scrapbook paper • white heart stickers • scissors • glue dots • hole punch • 1½" (4cm) metal fasteners • ¼" (6mm) wide ribbon

1 Photocopy the invitation template (found in the Templates section) as many times as needed. Cut out each invitation and fill in the information for your specific event.

2 Cut out a 5" (13cm) circle from red scrapbook paper, and randomly place white heart stickers on it to look like polka dots. Cut the red circle in half to create two "wings" for your ladybug.

3 Using black scrapbook paper and a 3" (8cm) circle punch, punch out plain circles for your ladybugs' heads. Line up the three layers of your invitation (from back to front): the black circle, the invitation and red wings (with the top of the two wings overlapping by about ⅔" [17mm]).

4 Holding the layers together, use a single hole punch to put a hole in all three layers. Use a metal fastener to hold all three layers together.

5 Tie a small bow with ¼" (6mm) wide ribbon and attach to the top of the fastener for embellishment.

DESSERTS *and* DETAILS

Nothing completes a party like a delicious selection of desserts! A few holiday favorites will delight your guests, while adding to the décor of your party table. Red gumballs, heart-shaped lollipops and conversation hearts are a great addition to our little love bug cupcakes. Don't forget to offer your guests a nice glass of milk to wash down the goodies, dressed up with a sweet straw!

Valentine Mailboxes
If you plan on having the children make or exchange Valentines at the party, hang decorative "mailboxes" on the back of each of their chairs. Try embellishing oversized envelopes with ribbon, rickrack or trim. Personalize them for your guests with markers or puffy paint.

◀ Cello Bag Toppers Party Favor
You can get very creative when packing candy to send home with your guests. Use the green polka dot cello topper template (found in the Templates section) to dress up your cellophane bags. Simply photocopy the template (one for each guest), cut out, fold in half and attach to the top of the bag with double-stick tape.

◀ Straw Flags
Milk is a fabulous drink option to serve to children, especially when accompanied by sweets. Dress up your milk glasses with a paper straw covered in hearts and embellished with a straw flag (found in the Templates section). To use them, print the template onto label paper, cut out, wrap around a straw and stick the two ends together.

LOVE BUG CUPCAKES

Cupcakes are a go-to party dessert. Extremely versatile, you can alter the look of our basic vanilla cupcake recipe (found in Chapter 7) for each individual party theme. For the Love Bug Valentine's Day party, take basic vanilla cupcakes and transform them into ladybugs complete with wings and antennas.

INGREDIENTS

vanilla cupcakes

white buttercream frosting

red food coloring

green licorice strings

heart sprinkles

white ball sprinkles

marshmallows

DIRECTIONS

After you bake your vanilla cupcakes, slice the top off using a serrated bread knife. Slice the tops in half and set aside; these will be your ladybug's wings.

Frost the cupcakes with white buttercream frosting. Using food coloring, dye the remaining frosting a deep red. Frost the top halves ("wing" pieces) with the red frosting, and add white ball sprinkles to look like spots. Place two "wings" atop each frosted cupcake at a slight angle so the wings are spread apart.

Cut a marshmallow in half and place at the top point of the wings on the cupcake. Use heart sprinkles as eyes, and cut green licorice into 1" (3cm) pieces to use as antennas.

Activity: Decorating Valentines
Set up a craft station with paper, stickers, sequins and trims to create valentines to exchange with each other and bring home to their family. You can purchase precut heart-shaped cards, making your prep work that much easier.

Chocolate XO Tic Tac Toe
Entertain your guests with a Tic Tac Toe tournament, reinvented with washi tape and chocolate game pieces.

Use patterned washi tape to set up the game board on either a white tablecloth or pieces of poster board. The game pieces can be made using chocolate melts and X and O chocolate molds.

resources

Paper goods, Cake Plate Clings (whhostess.com); red circle paper for invitation, heart-shaped paper for valentines, over-sized white envelopes (paper-source.com); metal fasteners, ribbon for invitations, 11" (28cm) lollipop sticks (michaels.com); felt, puffy paint for place mats (hobby-lobby.com); white pots, red striped glasses (ikea.com); heart-patterned paper straws, black chevron washi tape (shopsweetlulu.com); heart-shaped balloons, red heart polka dot balloons (partycity.com); wheat grass plants (wholefoods.com); red gumballs (candywarehouse.com); X and O chocolate molds (amazon.com).

XO Party Favor
Send your guests home with supplies for their very own XO Tic Tac Toe tournament: a roll of washi tape, and chocolate X's and O's. Package the items up in a cellophane bag and tie with a big red bow.

12

TRICK OR TREAT

after-school halloween party

HALLOWEEN IS ONE OF THOSE HOLIDAYS that evokes happy childhood memories for me, including colorful costumes, festive school parties and trick or treating in the neighborhood. It's an ideal time to host an after-school party, offering a quick snack for the kids and an opportunity to chat with the parents before trick or treating commences.

This chapter is full of ideas for creative desserts that could be used as a school treat or as part of a party spread. It also includes a couple of creative DIY projects and a few "tricks" that will make you the most stylish mom on the block.

SETTING *the* THEME

Simplify your party plans and style with just one fabulous table that includes your sweets, drinks and party favors.

Add a touch of modern glam to a traditional orange and black color palette by infusing silver accents into your design. I used the console in my living room to hold all of my goodies. The tabletop held the main sweets, while the shelves below held the drink options and party favors. I covered the top of the console with a hand-painted burlap runner. Layering different-sized black paper fans created a backdrop, and the sides of the table were defined with a large, 36" (91cm) orange balloon that was draped with a DIY ribbon chain garland. A large metallic silver pumpkin held center stage, adding to the modern look.

I used a variety of silver, white and glass serving vessels, and wrapped the stems of my cake stands with a black fringe garland to add texture to the table. Desserts included orange Jello, cupcakes topped with chocolate spider webs, whoopie pies and brownie bites. The kids sipped on glasses of milk that were embellished with "eyes" made from black electrical tape, and I embellished a few different elements with silver glitter to add more shimmer to the table.

Metallic Pumpkins
Northing gives a pumpkin a modern feel like a quick coat of metallic spray paint. To continue the silver accents for this party, I sprayed my pumpkin a metallic silver color, and embellished it with a black and white striped ribbon.

Hand-Painted Burlap Runner
To add a touch of modern flair to my burlap table runner, I stenciled a black chevron pattern onto it with acrylic paint, and then frayed the edges.

Repurpose Furniture
Instead of adding an additional table into your already decorated home, try repurposing a piece of furniture that is already in place. I find that I use this console over and over again for parties. The shelves give me extra space for displaying my treats, and the lower shelves are great for little kids who can "grab and go" on their own.

Embellished Paper Fans
Layered paper fans are an inexpensive way to add a festive touch to any party. You can embellish them by adding a decorative accent to the centers. Using glittered-silver scrapbook paper and a 3" (8cm) circle punch, I created a simple addition to my black fans. This little addition to my décor added a touch of shimmer and a whole lot of style.

Trick or Treat Banner
Construct a banner using Greek key-clad letters. Simply cut out the letters and punch two holes at the top of each letter. String the letters onto ribbon to create a garland.

DESSERTS *and* DETAILS

A Touch of Shimmer

Mini spoons and forks are a fun accessory for individual sized desserts. Embellish your utensils with glitter, ribbon or washi tape. I dipped these mini wood spoon handles into craft glue and then into silver glitter. I love the touch of shimmer they added to the table.

Webbed Cupcakes

Top your basic cupcakes with spider webs made from chocolate. To make these, simply fill a piping bag with melted white chocolate and pipe the lines onto a piece of parchment paper. Allow the chocolate to cool completely before you remove them from the paper to place on your cupcakes.

Ghost Milk Glasses

A simple way to dress up your everyday glasses for a Halloween party is to use black electrical tape. You can create ghost eyes on milk glasses, pumpkin faces on orange Jello bowls, or spider webs on vanilla pudding cups. It's a simple, impermanent addition to your party.

Glittered Gift Tags

As a child, seeing your name on a party favor or gift is a big delight. Dress up your basic party favor bags with kraft paper tags dipped in glitter.

RIBBON CHAIN GARLAND

Reinvent the traditional paper chain garland with this fresh update. Using pieces of patterned ribbons in my color palette and double-stick tape, I created this garland in no time flat. It's very lightweight, so you can hang it virtually anywhere. I love it hanging as a decoration from the jumbo balloons!

SUPPLIES

3–5 different patterned ribbons (3" [8cm] wide) • double-stick tape or glue dots • scissors

1 Cut the ribbon into 5" (13cm) strips.

2 Make a loop with one piece of ribbon and attach the ends with a piece of double-stick tape or glue dots. Repeat with another piece of ribbon, this time looping it through your first loop before attaching the ends with tape.

3 Keep alternating patterns of the ribbon as you continue to build your garland.

HALLOWEEN WHOOPIE PIE

Whoopie pies are a little chocolate cake sandwich with a creamy filling—a timeless treat that can be embellished for any holiday or theme party. Add Halloween sprinkles to this whoopie pie recipe to make them party-ready.

Whoopie Pie Cake

INGREDIENTS

3 cups (675g) granulated sugar

2¹/₂ sticks (275g) butter

4 eggs

¹/₃ cup (75mL) vegetable oil

1 tbsp vanilla extract

6 cups (675g) all-purpose flour

2 cups (175g) unsweetened cocoa powder

1 tsp. baking powder

1 tbsp. baking soda

1 tsp. salt

3 cups (1.25 pint) milk

DIRECTIONS

Preheat oven to 350°F (180°C or gas mark 4).

In the bowl of your stand mixer, beat together sugar, butter and eggs until combined. Add the vegetable oil and vanilla extract and mix again.

In a separate bowl, combine all of the dry ingredients and begin to slowly add to the egg mixture. Continue beating until the ingredients are well combined. Slowly start incorporating the milk into the bowl as you continue to mix on a slow speed.

Using an ice cream scoop (for consistent size), scoop out an even number of scoops onto a baking sheet. Bake for 10–12 minutes. Let cool completely before filling.

Whoopie Pie Filling

INGREDIENTS

3 cups (450g) confectioners' sugar

1 cup (224g) shortening

1 cup (240mL) marshmallow fluff

1 pinch salt

¹/₃ cup (75mL) whole milk, at room temperature

Halloween sprinkles

DIRECTIONS

In the bowl of your electric mixer, combine all of the ingredients, except the milk and sprinkles. After everything is combined, add the whole milk to the bowl and beat well until you reach a creamy consistency.

Pipe the filling in between the cake cookies, and roll the sides in Halloween sprinkles.

resources

Paper goods (whhostess.com); ribbon, burlap fabric, silver glitter (hobbylobby.com); black paper fans, orange 36" (91cm) balloon, black tissue paper fringe garland, mini wood spoons (shopsweetlulu.com); blown glass cake stands (williamyeoward.com); black and white candy sticks, orange candy (candywarehouse.com); silver scrapbook paper (michaels.com); orange bags and kraft paper tags (amazon.com).

To use this section, color copy the provided templates onto white paper or cardstock as many times as desired. All templates are shown at full size.

CELEBRITY
BABY NAME GAME

NAME MY MAMA!

___ CAMDEN JACK		A. REESE WITHERSPOON
___ APPLE BLYTHE		B. BEYONCE
___ GEORGE ALEXANDER		C. NICOLE KIDMAN
___ SURI		D. CHRISTIE BRINKLEY
___ HARLOW WINTER		E. JENNIFER GARNER
___ PENELOPE SCOTLAND		F. KRISTIN CAVALLARI
___ LIAM AARON		G. MICHELLE WILLIAMS
___ SERAPHINA ROSE		H. KATIE HOLMES
___ BLUE IVY		I. GWYNETH PALTROW
___ COCO RILEY		J. ANGELINA JOLIE
___ TENNESSEE JAMES		K. GIULIANA RANCIC
___ SAILOR LEE		L. COURTENEY COX
___ MADDOX		M. NICOLE RITCHIE
___ PHINNAEUS WALTER		N. TORI SPELLING
___ MATILDA ROSE		O. KATE MIDDLETON
___ EDWARD DUKE		P. KOURTNEY KARDASHIAN
___ FAITH MARGARET		Q. JULIA ROBERTS

Baby Chic Baby Shower
Celebrity Name Game Card

Answer Key (top to bottom):
F, I, O, H, M P, N, E, B, L, A, D, J, Q, G, K, C

Baby Chic Baby Shower
Food Tent Card (at right)
Straw Flags (below)
Rattle Placecard (bottom)

What Will It Bee? Baby Shower
Menu Card Template (at left)
Baby Bingo Template (top)
Honeycomb Placecard (at right)

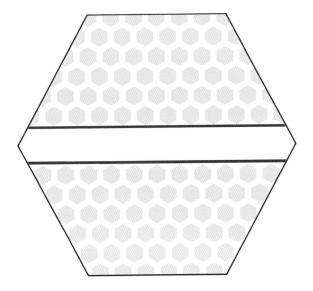

join us to celebrate!

for:

_____

date & time:

_____

location:

_____

please respond to:

_____

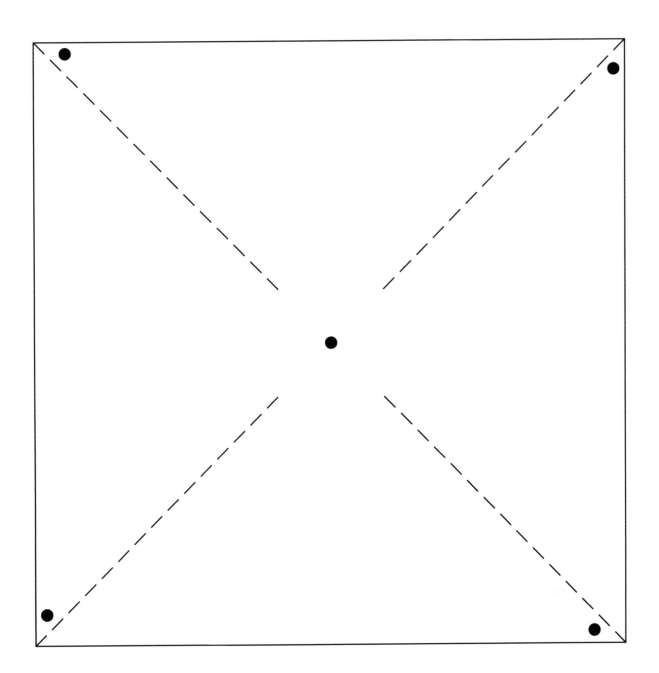

Pinwheels and Polka Dots First Birthday Party
Invitation (at left)
Pinwheel Template (above)

THANKS
for celebrating at
MUSTACHE
BASH!

Little Man First Birthday Party
Favor Label (above)
Garland Templates (at right)

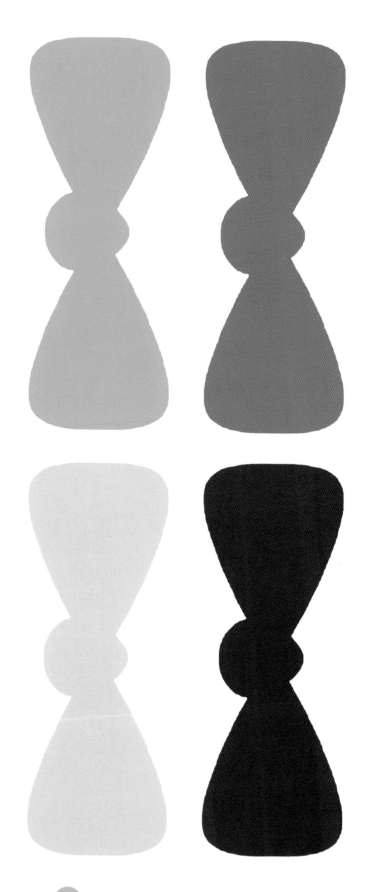

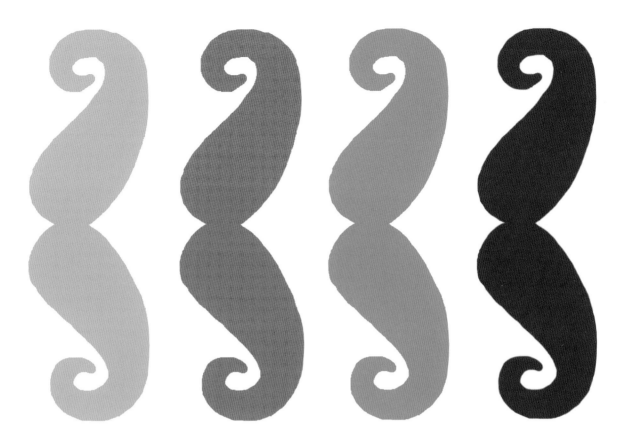

Little Man First Birthday Party

Garland Templates (above)

Modern Silhouette Birthday Party

Centerpiece Stick (at left above)

Gift Tag (at right above)

Modern Silhouette Birthday Party

Party Hat Template: Photocopy or trace onto patterned paper.

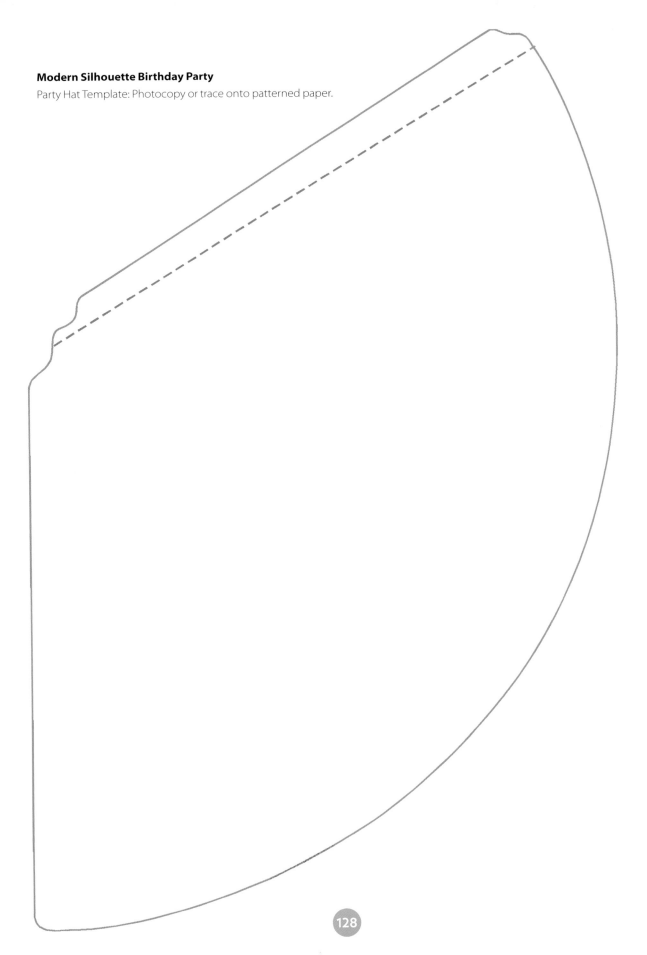

AHOY!

JOIN US TO CELEBRATE OUR LITTLE SAILOR!

WHO: _____

DATE & TIME: _____

LOCATION: _____

RSVP: _____

Classic Nautical Birthday Party

Invitation (above)

THANKS
⚓ for sailing over ⚓
TO CELEBRATE WITH US!

Classic Nautical Birthday Party
Rice Cereal Treat Sail Templates (top)
Thank You Label (above)
Invitation Anchor Cutout (at right)

Classic Nautical Birthday Party

Garland Template, Nautical Flags
(additional flags on following pages)

Classic Nautical Birthday Party
Garland Template, Nautical Flags

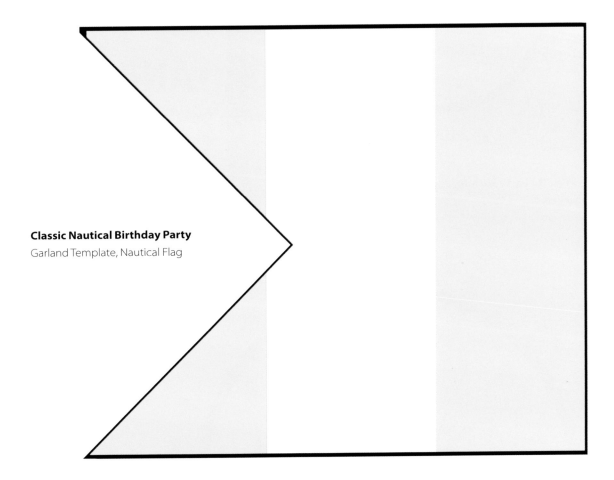

Classic Nautical Birthday Party
Garland Template, Nautical Flag

Formal Tea Party Birthday Party
Thank You Tag (above)
Circular Invitation Template (below)

Barnyard Bash Birthday Party
Animal Feed Label (above)

you're cordially invited for a

TEA PARTY

to celebrate with our birthday girl!

who: _____

date & time: _____

location: _____

reserve your table

rsvp _____

Fiesta! Birthday Party

Party Favor Paper Cone Template 1 of 2 (above)

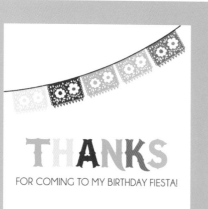

Fiesta! Birthday Party
Gift Tag Template (at left)
Party Favor Paper Cone Template 2 of 2 (below)

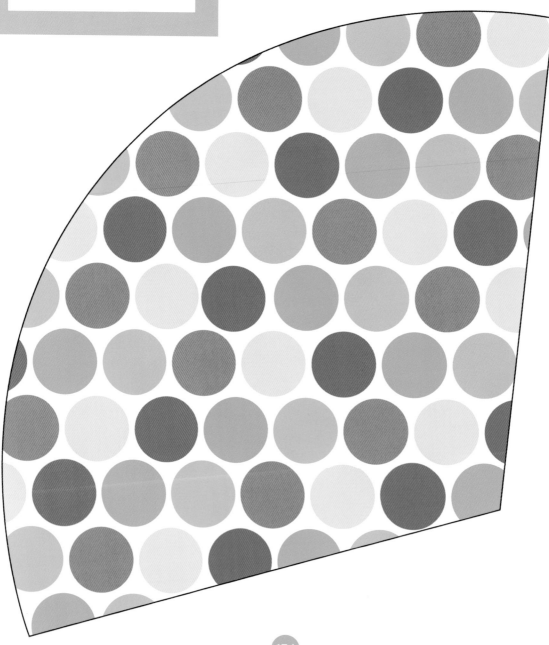

BIRTHDAY FIESTA

JOIN US TO CELEBRATE

WHO: _____

DATE & TIME: _____

LOCATION: _____

RSVP _____

Fiesta! Birthday Party

Invitation (above)

Golf Classic Birthday Party

Water Bottle Label (at left)
Food Tent Card (at right, top)
Gift Tag (at right, bottom)
Cupcake Flags (middle)

THANKS
for teeing off with me!

PAR TEE

LITTLE LOVE BUG

JOIN OUR LITTLE

LOVE BUGS

FOR SWEET TREATS & FUN TO CELEBRATE

VALENTINE'S DAY!

WHO: _____
DATE & TIME: _____
LOCATION: _____

RSVP:

_____

HAPPY VALENTINE'S DAY

Love Bug Soirée Valentine's Day Party

Party Favor Bag Label (at left, bottom)

Straw Flag (at left, top)

Centerpiece (above)

Invitation (at right, top)

ABOUT *the* AUTHOR

Kelly Rohlfs Lyden is known for her updated, yet classic style, with a touch of preppy pizzazz. Readers crave her fresh party style and flock daily to her lifestyle and entertaining blog, *The Party Dress*, for inspiration.

Her social stationery company, WH Hostess, translates modern, fresh designs onto paper and gifts. The growing popularity of the company comes in part due to creative children's birthday party collections. A classic approach to designing parties around a character or icon, such as a little blue car, a train or bumblebee look fresh when combined with modern, geometric patterns and trendy color palettes. Kelly pulls in elements that you would typically see at adult events, but effortlessly executes the design in a way that appeals to children.

In 2012, Kelly Lyden created the patent-pending product, Cake Plate Clings—a series of decorative linings designed for cake stands, pedestals and serving dishes. They offer a fresh, reusable update to the traditional disposable paper doilies and liners. Used for decoration under food, they are offered in vibrant colors and patterns from WH Hostess Social Stationery.

Stylish Kids' Parties is Kelly's first book, featuring unique, never seen before parties by WH Hostess, Social Stationery, DIY party ideas and more. Kelly is thrilled to have this opportunity to bring you even more party inspiration, and do what she loves best—styling kids' parties that put a smile on both kids' and parents' faces!

Kelly's work has been featured in *InStyle* magazine, *Stitch Craft Create* magazine and *Celebrate* magazine, as well as on *Martha Stewart*, HGTV.com, *Hostess with the Mostess*, *Amy Atlas* and countless party blogs.

thanks

The idea for this book was a dream that has lingered in the back of my head for quite some time—ever since I started designing kids' parties, to be honest. Turning this little dream into a reality took the support of some very special people.

I received the title of "Auntie Kelly" ten years ago when one of my best friends had her first child. Although I fell in love with the little guy right off the bat, I don't think I realized how important that particular role in my life would be. Ten years later, there are close to twenty-five kids in my life who refer to me and love me as "Auntie Kelly." Each one of them has made my life more joyful, and inspired one fabulous birthday celebration after another. Thank you to Kristin, Teresa, Sarah, Brooke, Casey, Beth, Barb and Sharon for bringing these special little ones into my life.

Thank you to my parents and family for always supporting my dreams and never telling me that I am crazy for following them. Thank you to my husband for putting up with my distraction over this last year, for listening to endless party ideas and only tuning me out half of the time, and for allowing me to explore this crazy world of entrepreneurship. I wouldn't be where I am today without your support.

Thank you to the wonderful team at F+W Media for making this a simple process. Specifically, Amelia Johanson, Kelly Biscopink and Julie Barnett helped to make this book such a beautiful finished product.

I could not ask for a better support system in my WH Hostess team. Thank you to Jennifer, Brittany and Dan for keeping that part of the business running smoothly while I was otherwise distracted.

Thank you to Sarah for being the best "support staff" a girl could ask for. She cut, glued, set up, cleaned up and helped me every step of the way.

Thank you to Teresa for arranging and hosting some of the parties and organizing such cute models.

Thank you to Angela for covering up my dark circles and making me feel beautiful during shoots!

Over the years, I have made some pretty amazing friends in the party world. I give my utmost gratitude to Jessie at Shop Sweet Lulu and Kim at The TomKat Studio for providing products; Candywarehouse.com for all of the delicious and gorgeous candy; and Sandy at Firefly Confections, Allyson at Allyson Jane Desserts, Lauren at Sweet Lauren Cakes, Lynlee at Lynlee's Petite Treats and Charynn at Two Sugar Babies for creating gorgeous cookies, cake pops and fondant creations for these parties.

A very special thank you to all of our darling party guests and models, and each of their mothers for participating in our colorful photo shoots. Teresa, Sarah, Brooke, Casey, Vana and Mary—thank you for taking time out of your busy lives to participate in these shoots. This book is even more special to me because your little ones are in it.

Benjamin: Thank you for joining our family this year, and for inspiring your Mommy's baby shower, "Baby Chic" (one of my favorite chapters in the book). I love you like crazy and I can't wait to help plan your birthday parties in the years to come!

Willard: Your enthusiasm for these photo shoots was somewhat unexpected and most appreciated. I loved watching you think creatively and offer suggestions for displays. Thank you for your help and for never saying no when I asked you to pose for a shot.

Emma Jane: Thank you for always enjoying the party! Whether we were celebrating Halloween in January, or throwing a summer fiesta party inside while it was snowing outside, you were always excited to be a part of the fun.

Mackenzie: My first goddaughter—you are the reason your Manny and I found "happily ever after," and for that you will always hold a special piece of my heart. I love watching you grow up and helping you celebrate every big milestone.

Caleb: You are a special little guy who continues to surprise me. Your first birthday party inspired me to start my company, and I love that I have been there to help celebrate every birthday since.

Olivia: My darling goddaughter—your sweet innocence and love of Auntie Kelly's "par-teeees" made you so much fun to have at these photo shoots. And your best friend, Penny, loves you too.

Sara Jane: My youngest goddaughter—I love being a part of your sweet little life. Thank you for all of the hugs and kisses and for being a part of this book. I promise to always be there to celebrate your big milestones!

Tess: Your spunky personality and love of a good lollipop always put a smile on my face and made our shoot so much fun. Thank you for having fun and being such a good big sister to Sara Jane.

John: Your first birthday shoot was one of the most memorable ones. Thank you for your big, toothy smiles and enthusiasm for that cake smash!

Marlowe: Sweet Marlowe, thank you for your excitement over a good tea party, a pretty party dress and an impromptu dance party. Your sweet, loving personality is one of the things I adore most about you!

Abby, Cole and Madeline: Thank you for your excitement to be part of the book. Your cute personalities and love of parties shine through in your photos!

Lastly, thank you to my blog readers who have been with me for more than four years now. Your support, encouragement and excitement over the years have energized me to create more and strive harder to inspire you daily. Thanks for following along on this journey with me.

INDEX

17 16 15 14 13   5 4 3 2 1

DISTRIBUTED IN CANADA BY FRASER DIRECT
100 Armstrong Avenue
Georgetown, ON, Canada L7G 5S4
Tel: (905) 877-4411

DISTRIBUTED IN THE U.K. AND EUROPE BY F+W MEDIA INTERNATIONAL
Brunel House, Newton Abbot, Devon, TQ12 4PU, England
Tel: (+44) 1626 323200, Fax: (+44) 1626 323319
Email: postmaster@davidandcharles.co.uk

DISTRIBUTED IN AUSTRALIA BY CAPRICORN LINK
P.O. Box 704, S. Windsor NSW, 2756 Australia
Tel: (02) 4577-3555

Edited by *Kelly M. Biscopink*
Designed by *Julie Barnett*
Production coordinated by *Greg Nock*
Photography by *Kelly Rohlfs Lyden*

www.fwmedia.com

metric conversion chart

to convert	to	multiply by
inches	centimeters	2.54
centimeters	inches	0.4
feet	centimeters	30.5
centimeters	feet	0.03
yards	meters	0.9
meters	yards	1.1

PARTY 'TIL YOU DROP!

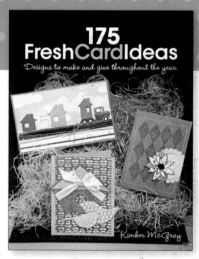

Make Me I'm Yours...Party

Create everything you need for a fabulous party on a budget with over 20 inspirational ideas. From cards to decorations to sweet treats, a talented team of contributing designers give you instructions and tips for creating your own fabulous party!

Silhouette Style

by Nanetta Banato

Silhouette designs take on color, dimension—and the 21st Century. Bring papercuts to life in more than 40 projects, such as tea-light lanterns, gift boxes, cards, paper dolls and fashion accessories, using papercut designs in themes such as sea life, animals, flowers and fashion.

175 Fresh Card Ideas

by Kimber McGray

Packed with ideas for all occasions—from kid-friendly themes and milestone birthdays to holidays, bridal and baby showers and sweet sentiments—you'll never be stuck without a design idea. More than 50 cards include step-by-step instructions, plus photo galleries provide even more inspiration.